MW00977044

Retail Fashion Manufacturing and Technology

by

Charles Nesbitt

Also by Charles Nesbitt

FUNDAMENTALS FOR SUCCESSFUL AND SUSTAINABLE FASHION BUYING AND MERCHANDISING
*
FUNDAMENTALS FOR FASHION RETAIL STRATEGY PLANNING AND IMPLEMENTATION
*
FUNDAMENTALS FOR FASHION RETAIL ARITHMETIC, ASSORTMENT PLANNING AND TRADING
*
FUNDAMENTALS OF FASHION RETAIL, TECHNOLOGY, MANUFACTURING AND SUPPLIER MANAGEMENT
*
THE COMPLETE JOURNAL OF FASHION RETAIL BUYING AND MERCHANDISING
*
RETAIL FASHION ARITHMETIC
*
RETAIL FASHION PROCUREMENT TEAM ROLES AND PROCESSES
*
RETAIL FASHION ASSORTMENT MERCHANDISE PLANNING AND TRADING
*
RETAIL FASHION SCENARIO AND STRATEGY PLANNING

Contents

PREFACE

The process of buying and selling in some form or other of goods has been with us since time immemorial. Often when one stands in bewilderment in an elegant shopping mall and wonder how all the stores are able to effectively seduce the many shoppers trawling the wide corridors to readily part with their well-earned money while at the same time enabling them to possibly enjoy a wonderful social experience.

The plan of offering goods to the potential customer is a complicated one and is a science that involves many players whose individual contributions slot seamlessly together and are so perfectly co-ordinated that it provides the perception that it is the result of one individual concerted effort.

It will be illustrated as to how the relationships of the major functions that intertwine from the conceptualisation of a product through to the presentation of a finished garment to the potential customer with particular focus on the technological and manufacturing aspects and in doing this demonstrates how the key areas such as buying, merchandising, technology, production, design, logistics and selling each with their unique specialised operations manage to achieve this.

The book endeavours to try and outline the basic key principles and mechanisms by which this happens and should be helpful to students, people in retailing and those who are maybe considering a career in the industry. For those who already are part of the fashion buying and merchandising community this book will be beneficial in that it provides a complete simplified overview of all the integral activities and roles that go to make up the topic and thereby will provide a broader insight into their own career.

The material of the book, other than that specifically referenced is the result of the author's own exposure to the subject during a career spanning thirty five years at a major retail organisation in Southern Africa, the support from colleagues, mentors, interaction with suppliers and own research. There has been some cross referencing to other books or technical material but the book focuses largely at a higher level on the key principles, concepts and theories and hence there is none or very little mention of retailers by name or technological packages for some key activities such as planning, allocating, critical path management, logistics and the like.

INTRODUCTION

Retailing

Retailing is the offer of goods or services for sale by individuals or businesses to an end user. The channels by which these goods reach the final user may vary considerably and arrive via different sources such as wholesalers, trading houses or directly from the manufacturer and there are equally many differing variants in the way the goods are put on sale. Historically it is more likely that shopping would have been done at the village or town market, in a high street shop or at the "mom and pop" store which evolved over time into mass retailing stores that are often housed in shopping malls supported by smaller line shops.

More recently with the advent of the computer utilising various platforms such as the internet or social networks, shopping on line is growing exponentially using electronic payment methods with delivery via the post or with a courier man knocking on the front door of the customer bearing their purchase relatively shortly after the transaction has been processed.

The products that are put on offer will be determined by the demand to satisfy a need in the market place. Broadly the merchandise may be categorized into food stuffs, hard or durable goods such as appliances, furniture and electronics and soft goods that have a limited life span typically clothing, apparel and fabrics. Whatever the nature of the product, the key objective will be to acquire and sell the product at a price that will be more than it cost to bring it to the place of offer and thereby make a profit.

Supporting activities such as the storage, movement of the goods, technology, and marketing will endeavour to ensure that the form, function and profit objective is maximised.

In an effort to put in perspective the activities and interaction between the various functional players and their dependency and integration with each other for the end to end process of the product workflow is broadly depicted in the diagram below

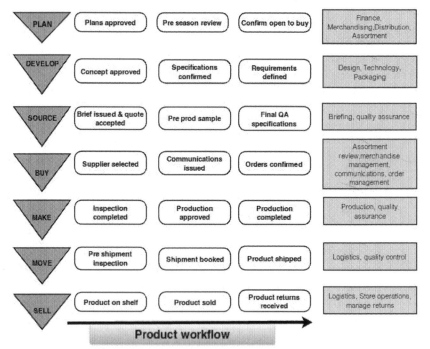

The distinction between supply chain and value chain should be clarified in that it is frequently misunderstood and the interpretation is varied.

Simply put, supply chain is the processes and activities that take place from conceptualisation of styles through to the procurement of raw materials and production process to the logistical operations and the eventual delivery to the end user. The value chain component is the inclusion of those functions that support the supply chain process such as the marketing philosophies. Human resource management, and consultancy resources.

The intimate details of the roles will be exposed in the future chapters as the science of retailing is explored in greater detail.

The retail players

The saying "no man is an island" holds true in many spheres and this is certainly the case in the world of clothing retailing.

Various players, each with very different specialised skills are amalgamated together to deliver a completed outcome which is that of presenting product for sale to potential customers. These players are often very diverse not only in the activities that they perform but also in their personality traits which they possess. The key to a successful team is how maturely the interaction takes place and the mutual respect that every member has for each other's roles.

Below is a brief synopsis of the main player's roles and their dependency and integration with each other. The intimate details of the roles will be exposed in the future chapters as the science of retailing is explored in greater detail.

THE PROCUREMENT TEAM

The foremost players in the clothing and apparel procurement team consist typically of the following members and are described in broad terms.

Designers

Designers have a deep insight into the market they are targeting through the analysis of the changing trends and use these to provide creative direction and develop product designs for the buying teams to consider.

Usually these participants tend to think out of the box and their creative minds can challenge some of the comfort zones of other team members. What must be kept top of mind is that they need to consistently apply their intellect way ahead of time as to what they think the customer requires as opposed to their personal desires.

Typically the character traits which they will possess are that they are independent, spontaneous, extroverts, driven by ideas and are confident by nature.

Although the general perception of the word "designer" conjures up a vision of those who work at couture level, the reality is that it also includes those who are involved in creating ranges which may also be exclusive but will be more widely available and therefore can be considered as having been mass produced. Their choices will be influenced by the type of retailer they work for or the product category that they design for. The more traditional retailer which serves predominantly mature customers will be less influenced by radical fashion swings which in contrast will definitely affect the younger market's high fashion boutiques more rigorously.

Work is done at times under enormous pressure to meet critical deadlines, tough meeting schedules and involves frequent international travel. It is not surprising the perception is often one that they live a life of glory and glamour but contrary to this belief the reality is that it is not as extravagant as made out to be.

The fashion and trade shows, whether they be for yarn, fabric or garments are tiring affairs requiring hard work and stamina as is the shopping for appropriate samples, researching fashion magazines, the use of forecasting trend agencies, internet and blogs and out of all of this they need to possess the ability to then distil the emerging trends to create a storybook that will best suit their organisation's customer profiles.

The designer lives with the constant strain of knowing that their level of success will be measured by the eventual amount of money rung up at the till and getting the styling direction wrong or overextending the life of a particular look could have severe financial implications, especially in the cases where volumes are high.

The real challenge is to convince the buying teams and senior management to buy into their vision and have the confidence that what they have in mind will be commercially acceptable to the customer. The designer cannot ignore the technical aspects of the garment production as many problems can be evaded if these are taken cognisance of during the design process. Retailers in the southern hemisphere do have the advantage that their seasons follow those of countries in the northern hemisphere which allows them to tap into the more successful designs that are trading in volume. However, with globalisation this is not always as clear cut as it was in previous years and the ability to follow as close to the season as possible requires techniques that facilitates the shortening of lead times and attempt to get the product to market as quickly as possible. The advent of communication technologies such as satellite television, internet and social media have brought exposure to different cultures, sports, films, lifestyles and trends such as those generated by specific events, health drives, environmental awareness and technology platforms that can have significant impacts on fashion which sometimes happen at very short notice.

A very important aspect is that the designer must adhere strictly to, is that of copyright. Instances have occurred that other competitor's garments are copied almost identically whether it be by style, print or design. Invariably the driving reason for this is the speed of being able to turn on a replica at a cheaper price. Although it may not be practical to register and copyright every design, any infringement can still be challenged and a consequence could occur of having the offending garments being removed from display and destroyed.

Buyers

The buyer needs to have a clear understanding of the product that is required which is in line with the trend guidelines best suited to their target customer profiles, for both the high fashion segment as well as those that best serve the more traditional customer.

It is a fact is that the role of the designer and the buyer may be a bit blurred in that they research the same fashion forecasting sites and other sources of inspiration in order to put a range of garments together. Both roles must be aware of sizing, quality and costs related to fabrics, trimmings and production. To achieve this successfully they must be flexible enough to develop and buy the most suitable product that is in line with the prescribed strategy and achieves the desired profit margin in keeping with the set down targets. The evaluation of competitive activity and product ranges through regular store visits and comparative shopping provides the knowledge required to keep ahead of the field.

Effective communication and presentation skills are a prerequisite to brief and interact with suppliers as well as presenting product reviews to colleagues within their own group at all levels of seniority. With this comes the need to be able to accept criticism and resolve problems in a mature manner. The sad fact is that frequently when the analysis of the success of the range is evaluated at the end of the season, if the results are disappointing it is not uncommon for the buyer to shoulder the emotional burden of the poor performance. The truth of the matter is that the range was presented on more than one occasion to all team players including senior management all of whom signed the range off but in the final analysis they are more often than not, as is human nature, reluctant to be accept any proper accountability.

Coupled to ability to understand the wants of the customer is the sourcing of the most suitable supplier that will be selected for the specified product types in terms of their particular skills, technical ability, costing efficiency, attitude, transparency, honesty, focus on quality, communications and competitiveness while still meeting the ethical criteria that are acceptable to society.

A large part of the task will be to maintain good relations with suppliers, while at the same time being able to assertively negotiate prices with them and make sure the planned stocks are delivered on time. Communications need to be clear and specific to avoid disputes over issues which may arise through vague and confusing messages. For these reasons they need to be confident, take decisions based on results and be driven by a sense of urgency.

The buyer has to be multi-talented in that as well as being creative they also need to monitor the sales objectively and be flexible enough to react accordingly in terms of turning on or turning off production and transferring fabric and components to more appealing product styles where sales performance and fast emerging trends dictate.

What is key to be a successful buyer is the ability to work as part of the overall team and influence the rest of the team's activities which could be in the form of a managerial and developmental capacity that could also include both their peers and superiors.

The display of emotional maturity and commercial acumen within the controlled parameters as set by the merchandising arm in terms of the budgets, the number of product options and display space constraints is absolutely essential.

The same principle applies to the relationships that need to be maintained with the technical teams in regard to the use of the most appropriate fabrics which meet the product form and function demands in addition to ensuring that the brand standards of the garment are observed.

The fact that potentially the buyer together with the other retail players will be dealing with three to four seasons simultaneously at different stages for each season makes their task even more complicated. To clarify the phenomenon a bit further, the journey of this book attempts to describe the process from beginning to end for one season but while trading in the current season the thoughts and strategies are being developed and documented for two or possibly three seasons ahead followed by the range development leading up to the production taking place for next upcoming season.

The ability to absorb and interpret vast amounts of information from various sources, much of which originates from complex IT systems, can present a challenge to those who are not analytically minded. Systems have altered the scope of the traditional buyer from being a pure "touchy feely art skill" to having to develop basic technical abilities through the continual emergence of innovative systems which have become a great advantage to the role.

Some buyer's, such as those for knitwear, ladies structured underwear, tailoring and footwear will require more expert fabric and garment construction knowledge of their respective industries in comparison to individuals who select the more straightforward cut, make and trim products such as dresses, blouses and casual trousers.

As the trade environment has become more global and through information technology development it is much faster, interactive and has enabled business to be done more effortlessly from a home base interacting with many different countries. A great deal of the job is done amongst many new emerging countries which has led to a need for urgency and nimbleness in order to locate the most effective plants that meet the quality requirements, be able to assess the required technical abilities, understand the economic and cultural demands of the respective countries as well as the logistical peculiarities and government regulations that may exist.

The sourcing of production has to take on different approaches as the pros and cons of dealing internationally needs to be carefully weighed up against those of dealing with the ever diminishing number of local suppliers. A critical factor is that suppliers must be ethical in terms of labour practices, remuneration, waste management, working conditions and safety. If such conditions are not met it is counter to the interests of the retailer to be associated with such suppliers from both a moral point of view and the exposure of malpractices could lead to negative media reports and the retailer will suffer the consequences that accompany such deeds. The measurement of performance is therefore key to gauging the effectiveness of suppliers.

In larger organisations a buyer will probably be supported by an assistant or trainee buyer who will normally be a person who wishes to pursue a career in the field. They will be largely responsible for the organisation of the ranges, perform some clerical work whilst preparing products for garment reviews, monitoring the product development critical path and production milestones, liaising with suppliers and technology as well as deputising for the buyer when they are out of the office.

A point to note is that the relationship between buyers and suppliers often develops into more than a pure business association due to the fact that they spend much time travelling together and working closely with one another building ranges. Close familiar relationships frequently make it difficult to maintain a business like association for the mutual benefit of both parties and can cloud business decision making and judgment. The temptation of bribery and incentives in exchange for placing large orders may be desirous. For newer naïve buyers the rule that the supplier is not your friend should be firmly applied simply because they are more easily seduced by grandiose lunches and gifts as many have unfortunately found out the hard way when they move on and are no longer of great importance to the particular supplier.

A way of balancing the workloads or ranking of buyers and merchandisers is to evaluate the actual number of suppliers, stock keeping units or barcodes being handled by each buyer and then make comparisons regarding workload and productivity of each buyer to established benchmarks.

Merchandisers

There is a novelty t-shirt on the market which has the following statement blazon across the front panel which reads as follows – *"Merchandise Planner – we do precision guesswork based on unreliable data by those of questionable knowledge"*. Although the humour can be appreciated it should be known that this statement is not too far from the truth as the success of merchandising objectives is reliant on many diverse inputs.

The merchandiser or planner applies their focus on maximising profitability from the business end. This is done largely through the analysis of historical sales and the influence of the trend direction to determine the range categories and product breakdown within the overall sales budget.

The role defines what stock levels are required to meet the preset targets such as seasonal stock turnover or forward stock covers based on the sales trends over time. Knowing these requirements, the merchandiser will determine what intake or purchase quantities are needed at any point in time in the season for the total department and each product category. The level of the budgets will determine the quantity of options in relation to styling, colour palette, size spans, pricing structure and levels of quality per category that will best service the customer for the time that the goods are expected be on offer prior to a new variety of product being introduced in line with the strategic predetermined seasonal themes.

The merchandiser's job has to be to provide guidance to the buyer to procure within the budget parameters. In short it can be described as providing the buyer with a shopping list or range plan that allows them to go out and fill in the blanks on the plan while buying product. This activity requires the careful management of the "open to buy" which can often be a source of tension between the buyer who always tends to want more and the merchandiser who holds the purse strings. A good deal of emotional maturity and teamwork on both sides is therefore critical for a successful partnership.

Sadly the merchandising role is often branded as a dull, boring number crunching task in accordance with mathematical calculations and while it is this, it can be better described as a creative manipulation of numbers. This task is highly rewarding when positive trade results are achieved or alternatively equally as depressing when these do not materialise. The role can be likened to that of a husband who places his entire salary on a dead cert horse at the races which was by no means appreciated by his wife. However when the horse won he was similarly unpopular for not putting more money on the horse!

Like the buying role, the merchandiser deals with different activities simultaneously as part of the team across a number of seasons and therefore requires high levels of multi-tasking and re-prioritising in the forward planning, problem resolution, critical milestone management, analysis and timeous action implementation.

As the actual trade takes place the results need to be carefully analysed and immediate action plans initiated in order to maximise the opportunities and minimise the levels of markdowns that erode the profits. For these reasons they need to be logical, reliable, and consistent in order to take decisions based on fact.

The regular timeous generation of reports detailing sales analysis, stock levels and forward planning needs are distributed to all team members and to senior management. Often numeric information and commercial analysis is demanded on an immediate ad-hoc basis which adds pressure to the job function and can be very disruptive to routines which in such situations requires the merchandiser to adapt quickly and effectively.

The merchandiser plays an integral role during the presentation at product reviews from the numbers perspective which influences the agreed product mix and justification of the levels of sales budgets.

A detailed understanding is necessary of the stores and the customer profile inherent to respective stores that are best met through the attributes of the ranges in terms of styling, colour and size that are put on offer within the store space constraints. The task is best described by the saying "plan each store as if it is your own" which could never be truer.

With sophisticated IT development and the availability of various software packages, some of which may be developed exclusively for the retailer, will provide quick sales analysis, production planning and afford the ability to make sound decisions based on accurate data. This information is especially necessary to give guidance to the allocator or distributor who will be sending the appropriate quantities to satisfy the store's needs as well as give direction as to the level of repeat buys for products that are trading above expectations.

Some organisational structures do differentiate the allocation function between the merchandiser who focuses on the forecasting and production planning and that of the allocator or location planner who will be responsible to distribute the product to the stores in the most appropriate combinations of styles, colour and sizes that meet the store profiles. This function can be housed as an extension within the buying division or may be part of a separate centralised group where an allocator may be responsible for a diverse number of departments. The benefits of such a centralised structure is that there could be a cost saving advantage especially where smaller departments do not warrant a dedicated staff member but added to this is a pool of knowledge which develops a highly skilled team who are able to cross pollinate information, coordinate inter departmental promotions effectively and develop consistent techniques and skills. The identification of common emerging trends will contribute to the optimisation of sales and assist in the control of stock quantities at a very detailed level and thereby maximise profits. Close connections to the departmental merchandisers is maintained to ensure that their actions are aligned to the departmental strategy and plans.

The need for the diversification of the function also makes more sense from the point of view in that where the distribution function is retained within the department it inevitably adds to the increasing workload of the merchandiser. The departmental merchandiser task has more and more been impacted on by the development, the implementation and mastering of complex and sophisticated information systems that analyse sales and stock with added forward planning functionalities.

Many such systems are able to integrate with other supporting IT platforms such as supplier performance, technological measurement, critical path management, ordering, logistical and store systems. The added management of a complex allocation system that is necessary to move the stock to stores is more and more difficult with the result that the incumbent is in danger of being drawn into concentrating on and coping with the intricate detail. As a result, the merchandiser runs the risk of losing sight of the bigger objectives as set out in the strategy and operational plans and the consequent degrading of the inherent merchant intuition becomes very real.

The merchandiser needs to effectively manage and develop the merchandising team which can, not unlike the buying role, consist of an assistant merchandiser or trainee who aspire to be a merchandiser.

The role ensures cohesion of activities that have to be synchronized based on actual sales performance through the formalised interaction with other stakeholders such as the buyers and technologists. This contact is usually in the form of regular, typically weekly, departmental meetings where corrective decisions and plans of action are agreed. Frequent association with the points of sale in stores through written communications and reports as well as formal site visits are critical to keep aligned with the customer's preferences and emerging trends and confirm that the stores are sharing the same vision of the overall strategy.

The need to guide suppliers assertively in terms of prioritisation and the achievement of deadlines is critical to meet the suitable stock requirements at any point in time, particularly in relation to peak seasonal periods or key events. For example, once winter breaks, which it does every year except the exact date is not easy to predict, the objective is to have the right stocks in place such as knitwear, thermal underwear, scarves and the like in sufficient quantities to meet the rush. The usual manner to assist in the anticipation of the weather trend is done through reference to previous years data when the weather changes happened which also help to understand variations in out of ordinary performance at particular times. The challenge is therefore to have the appropriate quantities in the stores at the vital time while the maintenance of the balance of stocks must be adequate to cater for the demand without overstocking the stores ahead of planned stock targets. Events such as Easter, Christmas, Valentine's Day and Mother's day are easier to predict and the right levels of stock can be made more accurately available at the right time.

Where suppliers do not meet the required delivery dates, the merchandiser needs to manage the consequences that have to be applied for the underperformance. This can result in some very sensitive and emotional discussions and the negotiation of penalties typically in the form of discounts, sale or return agreements or even total cancellation which will no doubt impact negatively on both parties.

Technology

Technical Teams consist broadly of the fabric and garment technologists. Fabric technologists are highly trained specialists who focus on typically woven or knitted disciplines. Specialised products such as knitwear, tailoring and footwear require added knowledge of components and specific production machinery.

A major portion of the fabric technologist's task is the development and innovation of new fabrics and the enhancement of existing products. New fibres and blends of fibres such as the blending of natural and synthetic fibres, addition of chemicals to finishing process will possibly lead to new inventions and improvements such as better washability, softer handles, easy care properties like easy to iron, crease resistant finishes, rot resistant applications, seamless or seams that are glued that allow for smoother looks particularly for under garments, the evolvement of elastane products such as lycra which revolutionised active and casual wear and the enhancement of thermal properties of winter undergarments. The success of such developments which add to the profitability as well as the form and function necessitates a close working relationship with suppliers, mills and value adders.

Garment technology have the responsibility to ensure that the make-up of the garment meets the set down criteria and the componentry like buttons, interlinings and threads are of the standard that is functional and are not inferior.

Many factories have developed specified technological capabilities that have been built around the production of a particular category of garments relevant to them which vary from factory to factory or even within the same plant. The garment technologist must understand this implicitly and exploit this knowledge to its fullest.

The relationship with the commercial team is sometimes strained as the ideal level of form and function can be challenged by the need to market the product at the most commercially competitive price.

The objective of the garment technologist is to ensure that quality is not compromised. The tasks essential to achieve this can be varied, for example, the assessment of potential manufacturers and fabric mills to ensure that the established standards are achievable, the specification of raw materials, overseeing sampling stages and ensuring that any delays which may result through the process do not compromise the delivery prerequisites.

In safeguarding that the all quality standards are met particularly through the inspection of garments, inspectors need to possess specific skills. Quality controllers should be ethical, sincere and honest, open mindedly being willing to consider alternatives, be diplomatic and tactful in their dealings with people and are able to actively observe their surroundings as well as perceive and adapt to varying situations.

The technologist has an intimate knowledge of the supplier base through historical awareness as well as from continually researching new and existing suppliers. As the sourcing specialist they have to guide buying teams in the selection of the most appropriate manufacturer for the various types of product. It is also very essential that they are conscious of the fabric prominence for the forthcoming season as dictated by the strategies and budget levels to ensure that there is sufficient capacities at the relevant mills to meet the overall demands without compromising quality.

The task of assessing potentially new suppliers is a role that may be included in the stable of the technical team or it may be hived off to defined sourcing specialists who are knowledgeable team members that recognise the strengths and weaknesses of suppliers and based on this where best to place orders accordingly.

Suppliers are assessed on various criteria such as their management infrastructure, financial stability, specialised equipment availability, fabric specialty, levels of innovation, fashion or basic production orientation, the other retailers they serve, their flexibility of cost negotiability and social responsibility policies. Other external factors that may well influence the selection of suppliers could be those like prevailing exchange rates, remuneration policies and physical locality.

In summary, the significance must be emphasised that the diverse buying teams all have to have a clear informed understanding of each other's roles and priorities and that they are aligned to ensure all their tasks are integrated to achieve the goal of delivering consistent quality products manufactured by appropriately skilled suppliers on time all the time. This is especially imperative in the case of more complex products such as corsetry, tailored garments and knitwear.

The handling, packaging, storage and movement of the product through the supply channels has to be done in such a way that the quality of the product is not allowed to deteriorate in any way whatsoever. As some product is sourced from more distant locations a newer trend is to contract the technical function out to approved independent technical service providers or to trusted garment and fabric suppliers themselves who understand and are committed to the standards required. These service providers are thereby able to approve samples, perform quality control and be responsible for the eventual release of the finished product.

TECHNOLOGY

Up to now the focus has been on the planning and buying infrastructure required to procure product and ensure the efficiencies that will enable the maximization of the profit opportunities. However this will not be entirely possible unless the product is as close to perfect in terms of meeting predetermined quality standards, the addition of new or innovative features, is safe and meets the ever changing social and global needs. These are the factors or pillars that underpin the very reason for the existence of technology.

Quality

A product achieves a high standard of quality if it presents well on display, fits well, wears well, washes well, is fit for purpose, offers value for money, is free from any defects, insufficiencies and is unhampered from deviance to standards.

The activities need to ensure that the product meets the stated design, technical tolerances, fit, and fabric and colour specifications. This is often easier said than done. Supplier capabilities must be freely available to achieve this as well as the fact that unclear communications of expectations and standards may result in specifications not being met due to time and cost pressures.

Innovation

In order that the offering remains competitive it is imperative that new features or attributes are implemented constantly. For this to happen it requires the continual investment in new, improved ways of developing and producing product or materials. Innovation may be related to the fabric, components, treatments, end product attributes, packaging or sources of supply.

Inventive construction can add value the garment in terms of form and function such as adjustable waistbands for improved comfort. The secure lock stitching of buttons and other small items on children's garments which reduce the possibility of them being swallowed. The use of especially engineered interlinings which have more resilience enable garments to be totally machine washable, for example in the case of men's suits.

Social and environmental responsibilities

In the modern day and age most people are very aware of the responsibilities that suppliers are required to meet in order to keep the world as sustainable as possible.

The use of organic fabrics like cotton that is derived from organically grown crops, the unsavoury practice of child labour in production process, the structures in place for the removal of chemical wastes and many others are issues which are continually challenged.

The evolution of production units in China initially did not see environmental awareness as a primary focus as they were more concerned with survival but as they have developed, the treatment of waste and use of electricity has become a more important factor to be considered and the laying down of guidelines and regulations have become the norm. Although the Chinese have become environmentally sensitive and implement environment protection measures there is still the tendency to focus more on the protection of personal health. The situation is in the process of slowly improving to protect other environmental factors largely due to the improved education standards of younger management.

The key points of attention for sustainable environment awareness is the measurement and constantly improving efforts to reduce electricity consumption with the reduction of energy targets in place and the use of solar panel technology or even something as simple as the siting of administration desks next to windows. The same applies to the reduced use of water and where possible the practice to use recycled water has been introduced.

Safety

The safety of the customer must always be paramount as there are volumes of examples of where people have been injured or worse due to unsafe or defective product. Technology should constantly strive to meet the highest standards of safety in their products as well as that of the plants in which they are manufactured and the logistical process that is followed in order to get the product to market. Where required, the customer should be fully informed of particular risks inherent to the products.

If supplier's products do not conform to safety regulations they are subject to risks particularly where the required certificates are not available to show that they have met the obligatory regulations. The standards should be documented on laboratory test reports and supported by the pre-production samples either completed by the retailer's technologists or an accredited independent third party external laboratory. In some of the large trusted suppliers there may be internal specialists who self-regulate this process but this may present a challenge where there is a broad range of product categories being manufactured.

Fabric Technology

In the buying arena an integral part of the role is a pre requisite knowledge of textiles and the beginning to end production process associated with garment creation. With a good understanding of fabrics the product appeal, value and innovation aspects can be maximised and the most appropriate material can be identified for a product that will deliver the required performance to best meet the end user requirements and expectations. The briefing and negotiating process with suppliers is also able to be conducted with greater authority and credibility.

Ongoing development of new fabrics is reliant on inputs from various sources such as that of designers, buyers, suppliers, mills, yarn providers as well as the dyestuff and chemical suppliers. A healthy interaction between the main players permit the fabric innovation decisions to be made earlier and consequentially enable quicker product development.

The understanding of fabrics enables the buying arm to maximise product appeal, develop innovative product, select the most suitable fabric for the product type which delivers the best performance for the end user and exceeds their expectations.

The production process using fibres converted to yarns together with processing through to the finished product can be outlined as follows

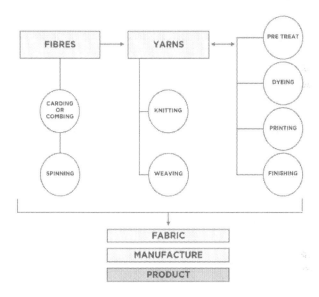

Fibres

The essential requirements for fibres to be spun into yarns is that it must be at least five millimetres in length and should be flexible and strong enough. Other inherent properties should include elasticity, fineness, uniformity, durability and a measure of lustre.

Fibres are either natural which tend to be predisposed to irregularities or synthetic that are more consistent and easier to control. Through the blending of both types in varying proportions it is possible to achieve a bit of the best of both worlds.

The continual developments of new and blends of fibres have transformed the performance of many fabrics particularly in terms of the form, function, safety and fashionability. Typical examples of this is the reduction of creasing and the evolvement of easy care properties.

Staple fibres which are of defined lengths are used for the construction of both natural and synthetic yarns whereas man-made filament fibres are extruded from natural gases and oil and stretched into continuous strands to manufacture synthetic yarns.

The properties of fibres vary dependent on the source.

- Natural fibres such as cotton absorb moisture well but need to be well prepared to counteract shrinkage, stretching, fading or being eaten by fish moths.
- Mercerised cotton has super aesthetics and handle and enables the achievement of deeper shades.
- Synthetic polyester has good easy to care properties, does not shrink or stretch and is economical but is not very absorbent.
- Acrylic is seen as a cheaper wool alternative which is moth proof but is prone to pilling.
- Viscose delivers a higher lustre with a soother softer handle.
- A blended combination of yarns from natural and synthetic parents take on the characteristics of both and the extent to which this is achieved is dependent on the combined proportions.

The different types of fibres that can be converted into yarns can be illustrated as follows

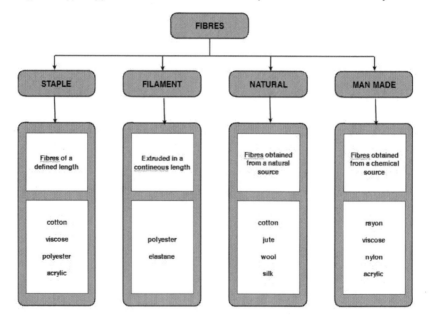

Yarns

Yarn is a continuous length of twisted or interlocked fibres which are used in the production of textiles, crocheting, knitting, weaving, embroidery, and rope making. There are two types being staple yarns that are spun from natural fibres and filament yarns which are derived from synthetic fibres.

Spinning of yarns may be of the same fibre or can be a blend of natural and synthetic fibres in varying proportions. The properties of warmth, lightness, durability or softness of handle can be achieved to a higher or lesser degree through the varying of the ratios in the blending in order to best utilise the positive characteristics of each fibre. An example is the polyester and cotton blend where the original cotton characteristics of softness and breathability are retained whilst the polyester offers the strength, wrinkle and mildew resistance.

Cotton yarns can either be combed whereby during the process a stronger and more luxurious yarn is created and the hairy surplus of the fibre is removed in comparison to carded yarns which have less body and are more hairy.

The different types of yarns, methodology of manufacture and properties are illustrated below

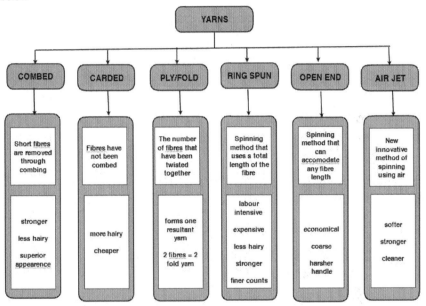

Yarn counts

Yarn count is a numerical measurement of the fineness of the yarn that denotes the relationship of the weight and length of yarn. As a rule, the finer the count, the more expensive is the fabric and it will be lighter if compared to like constructions with subjectively nicer handle and drape.

Sewing threads

Sewing threads are special kinds of yarn that are engineered and designed to pass rapidly through a sewing machine needle to efficiently form a stitch and to function without breaking for the life of a sewn product. The most commonly used fine fibres are cotton, nylon, polyester and rayon.

Fabric

Fabric is a flexible two dimensional material that consists of a network of natural or artificial fibres which are suitable for use in the production of clothes. The formation of the fabric is constructed through the interlacing of yarns known as weaving or in the case of knitting, it is the interloping of yarns.

Fabric blends are created to best utilise the positive characteristics of each fibre and the different fibres that are blended are usually natural and manmade fibres. For example a polyester cotton blend will retain the soft breathable properties of the cotton while polyester adds the strength, wrinkle free and mildew resistant features.

Fabric weight

The standard global measurement of fabric weight is grams per square metre (gsm). Factors that can influence the weight is the combination of yarns, yarn counts, knitting gauges, weaves and any finishes that are applied.

Knitted fabrics

Knitting is where the raw materials in the form of yarn are knitted into unfinished material commonly known as greige fabric. This is done by the use of needles that intermesh the yarn into loops. The weight of the fabric will be dependent of the yarn count as well as the gauge of the yarn. The foremost types of knitted fabrics are single jersey, ribs, interlock and fleece. The machines that knit can either be circular or flat in setup.

Circular machines do weft knitting which is where the yarns run horizontally across the width the fabric with the needles moving either collectively or individually to form loops.

Weft knitting configuration where the needles are laid across the needles in the weft or width of the fabric

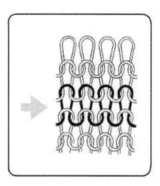

Flat knitting machines do warp knitting where the yarns run vertically through the length of the fabric and all the needles are used collectively to form the loops.

Warp knitting configuration where the yarns are laid across the length or the warp of the fabric. The loop structure is usually formed across two three needles.

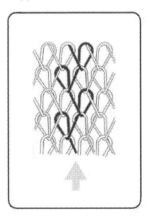

The gauge of the fabric is determined by the number of needles per inch and therefore the higher the number of needles the finer will be the fabric such as single jersey will the fewer the number of needles will deliver fabric such as knitwear.

Single Jersey fabrics

The common construction of single jersey fabrics is 24-28 gauge and have a weight of approximately 120-200 gsm. Single jersey is mostly used for products such as t-shirts, sleepwear, leggings and bedding.

The advantage is that it can be blended with other fabrics, such as elastane, has comfort as well as stretch, drapes well and is great value. The downsides are that it is prone to shrinkage and if blended with polyester it is likely to pill and have less absorbency.

Rib fabrics

The feature of ribbed fabric is that it displays plain and purl stitches along the course on both sides of the fabric and consists of alternating raised and depressed wales.

The characteristics of rib fabrics are that it offers better fit support, is warm as it traps air in the structure and drapes better than woven fabrics. However the finished fabric is generally more expensive than single jersey, has higher shrinkage than woven and because of the ridge structure it is difficult to print on. The finishing of the cuffs and waist bands need to be combined with elastane to function effectively. The fabric is commonly used for t-shirts and styled tops.

Interlock fabrics

Interlock fabrics are knitted on circular machines and the structure looks the same on the back and front of the fabric. It is a typical winter fabric and is commonly used for tracksuits and sleepwear.

The pros of interlock is that it is warmer than single jersey and is also heavier which gives it better thermal properties. It can be combined with viloft or Lycra and has better drape than woven material. The cons are that it shrinks more than woven, is unstable during processing and has poor recovery which is illustrated for example where garments may bag at the knees or stretch inconsistently.

Warp knits versus weft knits

Warp knits offer better stability with less shrinkage than wefts and commonly use synthetic yarns. They have a vertical stripe and are commonly used for swimwear, lace, mesh and net material.

Weft knits are used more often with natural fibres and have more stretch than warp knits. Stripes are horizontal and more often than not are used for t-shirts, fleece, underwear, sleepwear or tights.

Generally knitted garments are predominantly more casual, comfortable to wear and always stretchy, easy to wash, often wrinkle free and relatively inexpensive. Unfortunately they lack crispness and are not as dressy as woven, can shrink, stretch and lose shape and therefore can quickly look shabby and unflattering.

Woven fabrics

There are two main types of woven fabrics, namely plain or twill. Other woven fabrics include satins, sateen, dobby and jacquards.

The crisscross configuration of the warp and weft yarns to form the woven fabric is illustrated below

Plain weaves

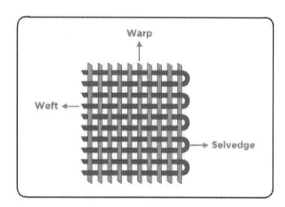

Plain weave is the most basic woven fabric where the warp and the weft are so aligned that they form a simple crisscross pattern such as in poplin, shirting and canvas where the thickness of the yarn determines the characteristic of the fabric. Plain weaves are mostly seen in shirts, shorts, sheeting and tablecloths.

While they are more affordable than other weaves and are generally more stable than knits but there can be a tendency for seam slippage or poor tear strength with lighter weights.

Twill weaves

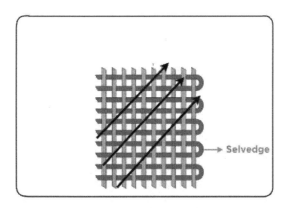

The twill weave differs to the plain weave in that the weft thread passes over one or more warp threads and then under one or more and so on. This type of weave is commonly used for chino trousers, denims, jackets, curtains and cushions.

Twill weaves have a defined face and more drape than plain weaves but are more prone to seam slippage.

Satins and sateen have a high lustre or shine where the satins utilise synthetic yarns, usually polyester, which can be either knitted or woven whereas sateen is made from natural short staple yarns such as cotton. The beauty of both satin and sateen is that they have a great visual appeal with a luxurious handle and is cool to wear. The downside is that they are difficult to manufacture and are prone to seam slippage and require appropriate machinery and needles.

Jacquard and dobby weaves are constructions that give special weave effects or surface interest where jacquard is more expensive to manufacture than dobby and is used to create complex design effects on the fabric surface such as that for jackets, curtains or table cloths. Dobby designs are simple weave effects and usually are used for shirting, bedding and tablecloths.

Overall woven fabrics appear crisper, are smarter, look pristine and seldom shrink or lose shape. They are, however, relatively more expensive than knits, not as soft and do not stretch which can make the garment feel restrictive in terms of comfort. Washing is more arduous or requires dry cleaning and the fabric wrinkles more easily.

While the warp yarns run lengthwise in the fabric and the weft yarns run across the width the fabric the fabric also has a face and a back with the face side having a better appearance which usually forms the outside of the garment.

Processing options

Greige fabrics require additional processing prior to being able to be made into a garment. Options such as pre-treatment, dying, printing and finishing are applied in order to improve the appearance, the handle, the addition of colour and patterns as well as the manual finishing such as brushing, and suedeing after the fabric after weaving or knitting is complete.

Pre-treatment

Pre-treatment consists of any process that is applied prior to any dying and printing is commenced. Typical pre- treatment includes the following.

Desizing is a chemical process to remove starch and oil from fabric.

Scouring is a washing process to remove impurities.

Bleaching consists of a chemical process to remove fibrous material such as cotton husk sand make the fabric whiter before dying, particularly for lighter colours.

Pre-heat setting stabilizes synthetic fabrics or fabrics containing spandex prior to dying.

Bio-polishing uses enzymes to remove hairiness, reduce pilling, improve appearance and enhance drape and handle.

Mercerizing is a chemical process whereby the use of a combination of caustic soda together with tension on cotton fabric to achieve brighter, more vibrant colours with a crisper smooth handle.

Dyeing

Dyeing colours fabrics though the dyeing of yarns, fibres or fabrics. The amount of dye required is dependent on the depth of the shade and the weight of the fabric requiring a mixture of water, dye, and an auxiliary such as salt or acid in order to facilitate the process.

The costs of dying varies dependent on the petro chemical market status, the depth or brightness of the shade required, the quality of dyestuffs utilised that meets the standards of light fastness, wash fastness and the environmental factors that need to be adhered to.

Continuous dying is where the fabric is fed continually through the dying machine and is usually the method applied for dying woven materials or garments such as chinos and sheeting. The advantage of this method of dyeing is that it is more cost effective for larger orders, accommodates crease free fabric and is a relatively quick process. However the negative is that there is relatively high wastage during the start-up and sampling process. Shades may also vary from one end of the fabric to the other through uneven penetration of dyestuffs and the handle tends to be quite harsh in relation to discontinuous dyeing processes.

Discontinuous dying is a stop start process whereby fixed quantity of fabric is dyed at one time in batches. Care needs to be taken to ensure that there is accurate colour matching between batches. This form of dyeing is used mainly for knitted fabrics where the fabric is allowed to shrink or stretch as there is less tension in comparison to woven fabrics. The process is cost effective for both large and small quantities and is commonly used for the dyeing of yarns where each yarn is dyed prior to weaving, for piece dyeing where the fabric is weaved before dyeing and completed garment dyeing.

Yarn dyeing has the advantage of better handling, aesthetics, and enables appealing crisp design in comparison to print especially for stripes and checks which can be equally attractive on both sides of the fabric. The downside is that it requires a considerable higher stock investments as each yarn needs to be dyed a different colour and minimum quantities usually apply. The manufacture of fabric is time intensive and requires a longer lead time and the fabric is not only more expensive than piece dyed fabric there is also a limited choice of colour especially from the East.

Piece dyeing has the advantage of having a shorter lead time than yarn dyeing and colour decisions can be taken later and deliver a softer handle. Disadvantage however is that it takes longer than continuous dyeing and the shade variations have to be carefully handled.

Garment dyeing is ideal for making colour decisions as close to the need as possible and tactics are developed whereby the base colours are held in stock and a quantity of undyed garments are held in readiness to dye in the ratios that the market dictates. Garments are usually informal and the colour and handle is very casual. Shrinkage is a factor that must be managed in the dyeing process and ensure that the end product is shrink free. Due to the fact that the batches are smaller and the process is slower the costs are generally higher with an added high reject rate as it is difficult to manage colour consistency across batches.

Printing

Textile printing is best described as the process of applying colour on fabric in definite patterns or designs which is not dissimilar to dyeing except that the colours are restricted to specific design requirements and is normally on only one side of the fabric.

There are certain considerations that need to be taken into account like the fact that the fabric needs to be prepared for printing through washing to remove excess starch and acids, the fabric must be absorbent as well as the need to ensure that the fabric is spun in order to safeguard that the surface is suitable for printing through the elimination of free fibres leaving the fabric as smooth as possible.

The correct choice of design is critical to the success of the print execution with regular communication between buying and the supplier or print provider in order that the expectations are met.

Cost of the printing is influenced by the size of the print where the bigger the panel or transfer print the more expensive it will be. The more colours that are utilised the more screens will be required and therefore the more costly it will be. The same principle applies to the greater the cover and special effects will add to the price.

The quality of the print is monitored by ensuring the registration is perfect through the accurate alignment of the screens, the coverage or thickness of the print paste is consistent to avoid variation of shades, the absence of short hairs or fibrillation will deliver smoother fabric and therefore higher standards. Other pitfalls that need to be avoided is the grinning through of the base fabric through the print design, or the cracking of the print deign when the material is stretched.

The performance of bulk testing such as wash, rub and light fastness after completion of the process is required to uphold standards.

As is the case with dyeing, there is two types of printing being discontinuous and continuous printing.

Discontinuous printing is in the form of panel and transfer printing.

Panel printing is in the case where the print is added to a panel or the garment and is typically used for t-shirts, sleep shirts and tracksuits.

The techniques of panel printing takes the following methods.

- **Spot colour printing** where solid areas of colour is applied for example used for character prints which are cheaper and quicker to reproduce.

- **Index printing** uses more tones to create more colours giving greater dimension which comes at a greater cost.
- **Simulated photographic printing** is the reproduction of photographs onto darker base ground colours which takes longer and is expensive.
- **The use of four colours, cyan, magenta, yellow and black for printing** enables the reproduction of photographs on lighter base fabrics.
- **Digital printing** is limited to size constraints and is relatively expensive.
- **Simulated printing** is utilised where the design resembles special effects such as embroidery or applique at a much reduced cost than the real effect.
- **High density printing** gives a three dimensional effect to the print where certain parts are raised. The downside is that it a slow process and is very expensive as specialised screens are required.
- **Spray effects** is where colours are sprayed onto the fabric and is typically used on denim and can be used in conjunction with a print making it quite costly.

Products that are used for panel prints are those that are water based for mostly lighter grounds, where chemical plastisol is used on darker grounds and gives a stiffer handle. Special effects are created whereby the fibre is dissolved leaving the polyester to be displayed but requires additional was treatment. Flocking delivers a velvet effect, while puff printing produces a raised three dimensional effect. Gel adds to a glossy effect and glitter delivers a shiny, sparkling effect.

Transfer printing follows the same process as panel printing except that the printing is applied to paper which is in turn applied to the garment, usually for logos, smaller prints on underwear and t-shirts during production through the use of a heat press. It is therefore more suitable for smaller prints. Transfer printing is also more cost effective and has the advantage that it does not have to be out sourced to an external printer.

Continuous printing is mostly rotary, flatbed or sublimation paper printing.

Rotary printing is the most common form of continuous printing through the use of roller screens where the ink is squeezed through the screens to form the design and is suitable for high volume runs. The number of screens is dependent on the complexity of designs, the number of tones, colours, effects and the machine capability in terms of the number of heads. It should be noted that the clarity and registration is more superior to flatbed machines.

Sublimation printing uses a continuous roll of paper which is applied to moving fabric via heat application and pressure through a two-step process whereby the paper is printed and then transferred onto the fabric. Rotary printing generates high definition but is restricted to polyester as it cannot be utilised for cotton bases and dyestuffs are used instead of inks.

The main techniques used in all types of continuous printing is commonly pigment, dispersive and reactive printing.

Pigment printing technique sits on top of woven or knitted fabric of any fibre type, and is the cheapest and most commonly available. It can be used together with reactive type of printing which produces a washed down casual look but runs the risk of creating a stiffer surface handle.

Sublimation and disperse printing techniques are achieved through a chemical process whereby dyestuff alters from solid form to gas through the application of heat and used to transfer a dyestuff into a polyester fibre either off paper in the case of sublimation printing or out of a direct paste for disperse printing. The advantages of this process is that it delivers a superior handle, is quicker than conventional printing, and is suitable for small production runs. Bright colours, with good colour fastness and easy care properties are characteristic but unfortunately it is more expensive than pigment and is restricted to polyester.

Reactive printing techniques can only be used on 100% cotton and viscose mostly for garments such as dresses, tops, sleepwear, underwear and leggings. That have better handle, stretch, absorbency, comfort and better seam appearance but is more expensive than pigment printing.

Finishing

Finishing, either chemical or mechanical is any process that is performed on yarn, fabric or product to improve the look, feel and performance.

This is done through the drying and stabilisation of fabric or the application of chemical finishes in order to soften in order to improve the sewability of the fabric, reduce creasing, prevention of microbial growth, prevention of seam slippage, make shower proof or manage the moisture which makes synthetics more comfortable to wear.

Mechanical finishes is that such as brushing or suedeing to provide a unique surface to the fabric that is good to handle. Sanforising reduces shrinkage on woven fabrics while compacting reduces shrinkage on knitted fabrics. Felting or milling is applied to woollen fabrics which creates a felt feel such as that used for melton jackets. Calendaring provides a shiny smooth surface while cropping reduces pilling through the reduction of the formation of hairy balls.

Denim is characterised by the yarn treatment where the inner core of the yarn is undyed while the outer core is the darker indigo dyed which lends to the fading properties as the outer core progressively gets exposed to the wear and tear. The harsh yarns are typically open end with the softer inner core being smoother combed yarn. Slub is purposely spun to look irregular with thick and thin places.

Denim fabric consists of blends with cotton generally blended with elastane to give stretch, polyester to give an element of shine, or all three yarns to provide stretch and shine. Fabrics are typically constructed as a plain or twill weave in weights of five to six ounces for shirting or bottoms at seven to fourteen ounces depending on seasonality.

The colour of the indigo varies from light to dark dependent on the amount of dye or the number of dips. The use of sulphur on top or bottom either gives black blue or blue black colouration.

Various washes are conducted in order to create different characteristics. These will include desize washes to remove the starch that has been applied for weaving, stone washing is very aggressive using a pumice stone to give distressed finish however enzyme washes are not as damaging as stone washing but the finish simulates that of stone wash. Bleach washing fades out the denim while sand blasting with a sand gun to cause abrasion while hand sanding creates a more gentle form of abrasion which will cause whiskers at the edges to give an aged look. Other types of washes are used to create creases or folds by using resins, snow washing is done with stones soaked in bleach which creates marble wash look. Tinting effects are created by lightly overdyeing the fabric such as a tea stain or orange tint effect.

Testing requirements

In order to uphold customer satisfaction certain key quality standards need to be maintained through the testing of elements of the fabrics. The tests performed can be separated into wet and dry processes.

Wet testing consists of stability tests that check the shrinkage of the fabric which does not impair the fit, the shape and the comfort of the garment, spirality tests measures the extent of side seam skewing after the garment has been washed. Wash tests determine if there is an unacceptable loss or bleeding of colour that will stain other garments in the wash load. Related to this would be the effect of leaving the garments damp in the wash such as cross staining of other products. Perspiration tests determine the potential of cross staining or discolouration of garments when exposed to perspiration. Light tests measure the effect of exposure to sun while chlorine and salt water testing checks for any reaction such as fading and cross staining to swimming pool or sea water.

Dry testing takes the form of abrasion testing to test for resistance to wear such as the knees of children's bottom garments. Pilling tests assess the susceptibility to little balls of fibres being formed on knitted and woven garments, tear strength tests measure the resistance to ripping of woven fabrics while tensile strength tests measure the amount of force required to rip or tear the fabric. Weight of fabric tests are performed to make sure the fabric is within the grams per square metre parameters of the specifications. Burst tests measure that can be applied on the fabric for example in the elbow area while the fabric slippage tests measure to what degree the seams can absorb pressure. Stretch and recovery tests ensure that the elastane properties perform as expected, dry rub tests measure the effect of the abrasion of two fabrics that are light and dark in colour, for example a pair of jeans and a white blouse.

PRODUCTION

During production it is important that the most suitable fabric is utilised to ensure the best performance of the product for the intended end use. What is equally significant is the specifications of all the components, make up and fit criteria and that benchmark quality tolerances or allowances are set to safeguard that the product meets all the form and function requirements. The responsibility for this aspect lies with garment technology and quality control.

Innovative garment construction is an integral part of the task of a garment technologist and many examples exist of creative inventions that have changed products to better serve the form and function of the garment. Examples include the modification of waist bands either by the inclusion of elastic which helps retain the shape of the waist or the waist ease design which provides for and adjustable waist bands that promote the comfort of the outerwear garment. Lingerie has also seen significant changes such as reinforced midriff panels in corsetry that enable smoother contour to seamless on sides of undergarments and the exclusion of elastic from leg opens which results in no visible panty lines under the outerwear garment. Bra technology is a science on its own and classic examples are the push up bra where especially designed foam profiles allow for better presentation of the cleavage, detachable straps facilitate the wearing of shoulder free and halter neck garments. Enhanced cup designs provide for smoother contour bras while the use of smart foam moulds perfectly and deliver the best vehicle for the ever popular t-shirt bra. A vast amount of work has been done in transforming traditionally dry cleanable products to being easy care and machine washable. This is achieved through the engineering of fabrics and components with durable fibres that are resilient and hard wearing.

A large part of the garment technology function is to match the technical capabilities and skills of the manufacturer to best benefit from commercial opportunities that may exist. Coupled to this would be the effective re-engineering of garments to capitalise on the cost saving aspect without the downgrading of the quality or performance of the product. The same objective can be strived for through the coaching and consulting with suppliers to review existing processes to improve efficiencies and achieve continuous improvement in fit and function of garments.

For these reasons regular manufacturer quality audits need to be conducted at both the assessment stage prior to production and also at any other time as deemed necessary in order to identify and prioritise any production risks as soon as possible. Such audits may take place in the movement of production to more appropriate suppliers, review existing suppliers that may be producing new kinds of products, ensure that the correct level of quality assurance exists where volumes have been increased significantly, the production of product for strategically critical launches or promotions involving marketing initiatives.

In order to minimise the risks that may negatively influence production it is best to identify production risks upfront, being completely aware as to exactly where goods are being produced or outsourced, that the critical path of management is closely monitored and managed and that a production schedule is easily visible and up to date with items being prioritised.

An example of a typical factory layout can be illustrated as follows which facilitates the free flow of material and operations in a structured way that alleviates the risk of congestion or bottle necks.

A simple example of the factory layout and flow

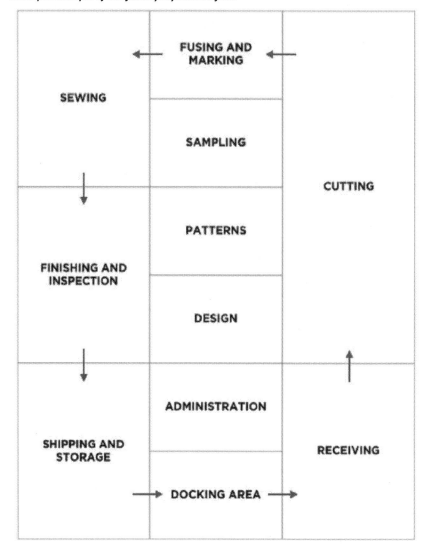

Manufacturing process

The process that is followed in the manufacture of a garment from beginning to end can be depicted as follows which is accommodated by the free flow factory design.

Drawing or sketch

An image of the concept for the garment is prepared to assist the pattern maker in understanding the style details required when constructing the patterns.

Basic block

A standard block with correct proportions is outlined by the pattern maker which is then used to construct a working pattern to be utilised by the sewing unit. The use of dummies in constructing the pattern provide an accurate base from which to work with clear direction in terms of fit and reduces the time spent on guess work. Patterns can be generated manually or computerised.

The stages of a blouse pattern development process may be illustrated as follows

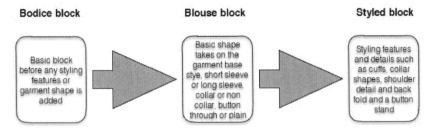

The benefits of standard blocks ensures the consistency of fit across different styles and particularly across different suppliers. It serves as a common base for pattern makers to work from, for example arm holes balance remain correct before any styling features are added, the shoulder slope remains the same across different styles and the minimum body over tolerances are set in place.

The pattern tolerances and allowances that need to be established are
- Over body tolerance is built into the fit of the garments to allow for movement within the size parameters.
- Shrinkage allowance is generally added to the width and length of the pattern which can vary according to the type of fabric and provision for any processing that takes place such as garment washing.
- Printing allowance is accommodated dependent on the size of the print, method of printing such as panel printing where extra allowance is added to the length and width of the pattern to accommodate shrinkage during the curing process.

Working pattern
Sample machinists require a base to create a garment which is presented in the form of a working pattern and may or may not be modified during the sampling process.

Sample making
The concept or representative idea is created from a working pattern to be assembled into garment form. This may not necessarily be done using the intended fabric in order to save costs but are primarily used to analyse the pattern fit and design. The sample is then reviewed by a panel of designers, pattern makers and sewing specialists who can recommend changes.

Costing
The fundamental cost structure is determined based on the fabric usage and the time taken to produce the garment known as the labour minute rating.

Production pattern
The final perfect pattern evolves from the working pattern and is used in bulk production. There are various tolerances and allowances that are accommodated for during the pattern make. Examples may be the over body tolerance which is built into the fit of the garment to allow ease of movement within the size parameters, a shrinkage allowance which is added to the pattern piece in the width and the length accommodates fabric shrinkage during printing.

Grading
The provision for the size spread is done by a pattern grader who creates patterns in different sizes by scaling the sample size, which is usually a middle size production pattern up or down. This may be done manually or by a computer. Production samples of the graded pattern samples are made and tested for fit and serve as a point of reference.

Marker making
Markers or the cutting plan are printed or drawn as an outline of the pattern parts onto paper that is the same width and length of the fabric which is positioned on top of the lay and held in place by weights. This is an essential step in the manufacture process as it serves as a guide for the operator during the cutting procedure. The function can be done manually or utilising a computerised marker package. Manual marking is time consuming, subject to errors such as overlapping poor definition and the accuracies are dependent on the operator's skill levels. The computerised process on the other hand is accurate, quicker, and determines the optimum usage of fabric. It can also be retained on record for future reference.

An illustration of the marking of patterns on the fabric lay on the cutting table

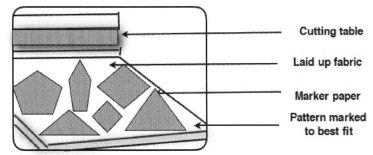

The rating or consumption is the actual amount of fabric required to cut a specific garment and the adequacy of a marker is the percentage of the fabric that is covered by the cut patterns. The less unused fabric which is not covered by the patterns, the higher is the efficiency as it should be remembered that the waste is still included in the cost of the garment. Other factors that influence the efficiency of fabric usage is different pile directions or one way characteristics, stripes or checks that need to match, border prints, size ratios and the number of units.

Some of the quality defects that need to be watched out for during the spreading operation is possible missing pattern parts, patterns facing the incorrect direction on napped fabrics such as velvets and those with different pile ways, mismatched stripes and checks, different fabric grains or where the line definition is poor.

Fabric spread

In order to prepare for the cutting process the fabric is spread out on tables. The extent of the lay will be calculated according to the marker and the number of lays which determines the lay height to meet the order plan of a specific contract. It is important that the fabric is inspected prior to and during spreading where it is confirmed that it meets the buyers requirements, does not shrink during steaming or fusing, bow or skew and is free from defects. It is also is measured to ensure that the fabric meets the specifications. This operation can be done either manually where the fabric is stared at the end of the table and the roll is moved backwards while the width edges are aligned, is free of tension and wrinkle. Automatic spreading is done utilising a machine where the operator stands on a platform while the fabric is spread and is then cut at the start of the table and then returns to lay the next ply.

Cutting

In preparation for cutting the fabric has to be withdrawn from a storage area where the fabric is stored in a cool environment off the floor in shelves or on palettes out of the way of direct sunlight which can cause discolouration of fabric.

The amount of fabric required is calculated by the ratings as achieved by the markers and before cutting can commence it has to be relaxed for twenty four hours.

The height of the lay should be such that it allows the easy manoeuvring of straight blades through the lay and preventing the possibility for the lay to shift in spite of weights being used to keep the paper markers in place.

During the laying process which may be done manually or by the utilisation of an automated spreader of the fabric it is important that the different dye lots are separated in order to avoid colour variations in the sewing process. The lays should not be too high otherwise the fabric may move during the cutting and a maximum height of eighteen centimetres is recommended.

In terms of laying up one way fabrics such as corduroys, stripes or checks this has to be done manually for matching.

Fusing is used commonly for collars, cuffs, facings, garment panels and waistbands utilising a machine that applies heat and pressure for the operation.

Where products need to be processed, for example garment washing, the quantities are set up in smaller lays to enable completed garments to be sent to the processor in manageable quantities.

The most common cutting process is done using a powered cutting machine suitable for the type of cloth. Portable straight blade machines are used for bigger garment components which has a vertical blade that reciprocates up and down and corners and curves can be cut accurately. The depth of the lay is dependent on the length of the blade and pieces cut from the lay will be identical. The portable round blade machine is however only able to cut in straight lines or very gentle curves. Such machines are very popular as they are fast and light. Stationery or fixed cutters such as the band knife contains a narrow, sharp endless blade and the fabric is pushed against the blade by hand where there is an air cushion below the pile to facilitate easy movement while following the markers.so that corners, tight curves and pointed incisions are cut precisely.

Other types of stationery cutters are the servo cutter which combines vertical cutting and a band knife into one machine with an overhead servo machine with adjustable speed and a knife that is suspended perpendicularly on a swivel arm. Metal die cutting where the die is placed on top of the material and is pressed through the fabric is mainly used for leathers coated and laminated materials.

Smaller parts such as collars and cuffs are cut using a band knife machine. For safety assurance it is imperative that metal gloves are worn when operating these machines

As technology has progressed in the modern age the cutting operation driven by computerized programmes have become more popular. This new technology lays the fabric on an air suction table which prevents movement of the lay which is uniform without excessive stretching and because is automated it requires fewer people, is much faster than the conventional cutting process and more accurate and therefore in the long term becomes cost efficient.

Other methods of stationery cutting is the use of plasma cutting which is the use of high temperature high velocity gas jets but does come with higher engineering and costs. Water jet cutting is achieved by high velocity of water in the form of a thin stream that tears the fires on impact and is best suited to fabric such as leather and plastic. The disadvantages that exist is the inconsistency, wet edges and high equipment costs.

Defects in the cutting process may consist of frayed, ragged or serrated edges and precision of patterns that eliminate over or under cutting.

Bundling

It is important that dye lots are be separated to avoid colour variations on panels when garments are sewn and therefore the cut panels are sorted into complete garments by size and separate dye lots. The grouping of these cut sections are numbered and then bundled ready to be sent to the sewing section.

Sewing

After the sorted bundles are received they can be stitched. For example, the sleeves, bodice and collars are assembled and stitched together to complete the final form of the garment.

It is important that certain elements are compatible with the fabric such as the stich type, machine with correct attachments and folders, needle type, seam and thread widths, all of which will contribute towards the appearance, functionality and cost of the garment.

As important is the operator skill levels that are necessary in terms of the core competence required with the appropriate experience in regard to abilities such as manual dexterity, finger dexterity, near vision, colour discrimination and the attention to detail.

In the sign off of the garment construction standards the guidelines that need to be followed are those dictated by the fittings, the pre-production samples and the final production samples.

The most common stitch types are:

Lock stitch which is used mainly in visible areas such as top stitching and on collars as well as for the insertion of zips.

*Over locking stitche*s are utilised to cover raw edges of exposed seams.

Safety stitches which are predominantly used for the joining seams mostly for woven and denim fabrics.

Mock safety stitches are also used for the joining of seams but mainly for knitted fabrics.

Chain stitch close seams of mainly woven and denim products.

Cover stitch is used in the main in undergarments to conceal elastics or to cover hems and can also serve as a decorative feature.

Blind stitches generally close hems on garments such as trousers or skirts.

Common defects that must be avoided in the sewing operation is needle and feed damage, skipped or broken stitches and seam grin or pucker.

The characteristics of a seam that is well constructed is that they are strong, durable, have a good relative elasticity, are secure and neat.

The performance of the seam will be influenced the weight, strength and durability of the fabric together with the seam construction, stitches per centimetre, strength and elasticity of thread used.

Specialised seaming such as darts, pleats, tucks, binding and piping as well as gauging require higher levels of operator skills.

The most common seam types are:

Plain seams are the simplest and used most often in various products from pillows to pants.

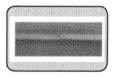

French seams have a clean finished look and are used successfully on high slippage fabrics which are susceptible to fraying and are also used with sheer materials to conceal the thread. Such seams are commonly employed on fabrics such as satin, sateen, voile and organza types.

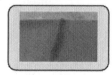

Lap or posted seams are used typically on bulky fabrics that do not ravel like leathers, felt and denim.

Bound seams provide a cleaner finish and aesthetic appeal on mainly light weight fabrics more often for silk or linings of jackets.

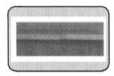

Blind seams deliver a neat appearance and prevent rough edges for products as in lined drapes, curtains, blinds and denim side seams.

Pleats, darts, tucks and gauging are at the best if they lie correctly with no distortion with secure stitching at the end, the marking of which should not be visible from the outside of garment and paired tucks must be equal in length and balanced.

Hems should be level if straight but if curved must be balanced without any twisting or roping and secure.

Binding and piping should be without roping or twisting, of consistent width and without visible joining. The fabric should not be visible through the binding and allow for adequate extensibility.

Collars require precise cutting of fabric and interlinings and should be accurately centred, balanced in the creation of the mirrored finished appearance.

Pockets need to have adequate width, depth and strength to effectively functional and where the corners are mitred, these should be equally balanced and where they are a styling feature they should be perfectly shaped, positioned with superior sewing detail.

Zips must be stitched clear of the coil of teeth to allow for the free ride of the slider.

Buttonholes need to be compatible with the size of the button with a stitch density that does not allow the buttonhole to fray away from the fabric which is mostly common on knitted garments where they may need to be reinforced with a woven interlining.

Buttons are attached with a secure lock stitch or chain stitch. Two buttonhole buttons should have the holes running horizontally and where there are four buttonholes buttons they should be attached with the holes facing square on.

Processed garments require stricter controls due to their nature to achieve the best end result. Particular attention needs to be given to thread selection which has to be stronger, the selection of fusing and wadding in jackets must be such that it will not delaminate or disintegrate and fabric shrinkage needs to be closely monitored so that the garment does not become distorted during the washing process and the extent of shrinkage is carefully monitored.

Ironing and finishing

After the sewing process is complete the final stage of finishing can take place where the garment will get its final look which may include some form of decoration like that of the stitching of a cuff, the addition of a pocket or emblems, buttons or Velcro snap fasteners.

The garment needs to be made neat and tidy through the removal of loose threads, fibre and fluff, elimination of stains and final checks are done which include the detection of needles for obvious safety reasons.

Pressing is an essential part of the garment presentation. The methods and equipment will be dependent on product and fabric type in order to achieve the desired garment appeal.

The finished garment is sent to the packing section where it is ticketed, labelled and packaged.

Inspection

Inspection of the product is done during the production process at each critical key point and the type of defects that are watched out for are open seams, incorrect stitching techniques, non-matching threads or improper creasing.

After production is complete the detection of defects is repeated but attention is also given to any possible colour mismatches, incorrect sizing of components, missing buttons and inappropriate trimmings.

Audits of quality standards take place at various stages and places to make sure that the best possible product is delivered. The audit process starts with the pre-production sample where all stakeholders agree on the standards that must be met to set the established benchmarks to which the end of line garments will be compared. Tolerances are set up front such as the percentage defects that will be accepted before a declaration of failure for each category of imperfections. Such declared tolerances will avoid future disputes in the event of whether or not a garment with defects qualifies as a reject.

Roving in line inspections also take place at various points during production for both measurement and construction to ensure the set criteria is being met.

The inspection points that take place during the garment production process can be illustrated as follows

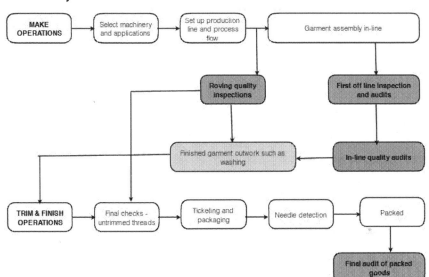

A zero defect would be where the imperfection could be a safety risk to the consumer like insecure studs or protruding metal ribbing in corsetry.

A serious defect is such that the consequence would result in product failure or render the product to be unsaleable as in the case of broken stitches, excessive grinning and holes.

Minor defects are classified where the product would still be useable but does not meet the acceptable standards like loose threads that could result in reduced sales. Other options of random testing may exist at picking and packing stage by either the retailer's representatives or an authorized agent.

It is important that a system is in place whereby it is ensured that reject garments are isolated, labels removed and clearly marked in order that they do not get included again with passed garments. The rate of rejects should be measured and analysed as an endeavour to minimise the failure rate.

Packing

The packing of the product is done according to specified techniques possibly using templates in such a way to ensure that the quality and integrity of the garment is maintained. Tagging with appropriate ticketing and promotional material is attached in accordance to the retailer's specification.

Cartons

Placing product into cartons is the final packing operation of the garment prior to shipment. The quantity per carton and the configuration within must be consistent. The labelling and markings on the carton has to be as per the regulatory requirements and as part of the quality check there should be a reconciliation of what the contents should be and what they actually are.

Sampling stages

Sampling takes place at different stages during the manufacturing process and serve differing purposes and in essence the main object is achieving absolute clarity in terms of what is expected in terms of styling, required quality standards, confirming the practicality of the patterns and getting the approval of the retailer.

The main types of samples that exist are the following:

Design concept sample is the very first sample which is developed by either the supplier or the retailer with the primary objective to get acceptance and decision to proceed with the garment.

Proto type sample which is prepared as the sample that accompanies the order and is frequently that sample which is utilised in initial range presentations which may or not be in the actual fabric and is really used acquaint those who need to progress further and changes may be made to some styling details, fit or trims and accessories.

Fit samples are made up in order that the buyer is able to confirm the fit on dummies or live models and check the garment for construction acceptability and should be in the fabric that is going to be used for bulk production.

Marketing sample is for use in the promotion of the garment and is used for photo shoots which would include the on line channel.

Size set samples for the buyer to assess that the garment fits properly across all sizes and will serve as a point of reference once production commences.

Technology sample is for technical tests to be conducted on such as wash tests for testing the feel and handling after washing, chemical and physical performance tests to ensure that they meet the required standards.

Pre-production sample is probably the most important sample as it is the signed off sample that is representative in all ways as to what can be expected in production and should there be any dispute during or after production it will serve as the point of reference.

Production sample is the first representative sample that comes off the production line and is sent to the buyer to confirm that it matches the pre-production sample.

Shipment sample is usually the sample received from off shore suppliers by the retailer to authorise the shipment of orders.

During the manufacturing process the pitfalls to be aware of can be depicted at the various stages as follows

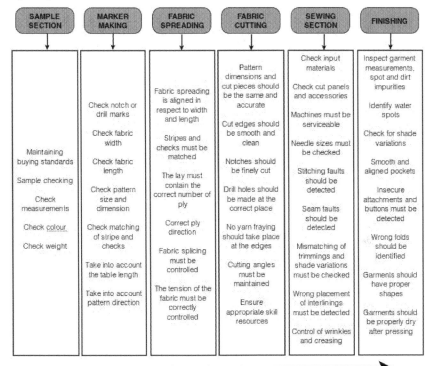

SAMPLE SECTION	MARKER MAKING	FABRIC SPREADING	FABRIC CUTTING	SEWING SECTION	FINISHING
Maintaining buying standards	Check notch or drill marks	Fabric spreading is aligned in respect to width and length	Pattern dimensions and cut pieces should be the same and accurate	Check input materials	Inspect garment measurements, spot and dirt impurities
Sample checking	Check fabric width	Stripes and checks must be matched	Cut edges should be smooth and clean	Check cut panels and accessories	Identify water spots
Check measurements	Check fabric length	The lay must contain the correct number of ply	Notches should be finely cut	Machines must be serviceable	Check for shade variations
Check colour	Check pattern size and dimension	Correct ply direction	Drill holes should be made at the correct place	Needle sizes must be checked	Smooth and aligned pockets
Check weight	Check matching of stripe and checks	Fabric splicing must be controlled	No yarn fraying should take place at the edges	Stitching faults should be detected	Insecure attachments and buttons must be detected
	Take into account the table length	The tension of the fabric must be correctly controlled	Cutting angles must be maintained	Seam faults should be detected	Wrong folds should be identified
	Take into account pattern direction		Ensure appropriate skill resources	Mismatching of trimmings and shade variations must be checked	Garments should have proper shapes
				Wrong placement of interlinings must be detected	Garments should be properly dry after pressing
				Control of wrinkles and creasing	

Production systems

The variety of configurations of the layout of sewing machine production lines can be set out in several ways and the selection of the most appropriate arrangement will be determined by the nature and quantity of product being manufactured.

Examples of typical optional configurations for a production line

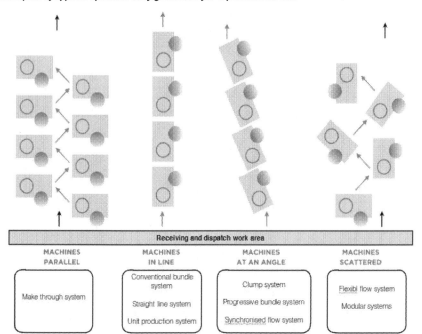

In the main the appropriate production system is set up based on the product style, types of machines and availability of the required operator skill level.

The layout of the equipment will also vary dependent on the nature of the product type in the factory and the system employed may well include the smooth integration of the material handling, production process and the personnel that will direct the workflow to deliver the finished product.

Make through system is one of the typical production systems that is generally used is the where one operator will do all the stages of the sewing operation from beginning to end and after completion will commence with the next garment. Although this is easy to supervise it delivers a comparatively low productivity and is dependent on highly experienced operators and therefore comes with a high labour cost. This type of format is suited to the manufacture of couture garments and sample making.

Conventional bundle system is also employed on a line system of sewing machines in a line configuration where work flows from a central areas to the first machine and then back to the next machine and so forth. The person stationed at the central area is responsible for the control of the work flow of the movement of the bundles.

Clump system is where the worker collects a clump of work from the work central area and completes a specific operation. After this is completed the clump is returned to the central area after which a second operator will collect the clump and complete the second operation and so it will carry on until the garment is finished.

Progressive bundle system is where the sewing operations are laid out in sequence. Each operator receives the bundle and completes their specific task and passes the bundle on via a container or conveyer belt to the next operator who performs the next task. This system is a very common method in many clothing factories these days typically in the case of shirt, jackets, and jeans.

Flexible flow systems is where the operators are positioned in such a way where the correct number of operators arranged in organised groups dependent on the each type of task and the layout is usually in a parallel formation planned in detail to ensure a balanced output until the garment is completed.

Straight line systems is similar in principle to the flexible flow system except each operation takes a similar time to complete and operators only handle one garment at a time. Garments will possibly pass from on work station to the next on a conveyer belt at a rate that is manageable.

Synchronised flow systems apply where the garments of a specific colour and size are passed from station to the next for assembly while components such as collars, cuffs and other features are done simultaneously down another line and at the end the two completed operations are brought together and processed to complete the garment.

Unit production system is a computer controlled production line where an overhead conveyer system move the product from one operation station to the next utilising a hanger carrier for assembly. The automated materials handling replaces the traditional method of bundling, tying, marking and manual movement of product. The advantage of the computerised aspect is that data gathering enables the productivity to be measured, establishing the input of information to the payroll and tracking of styles.

Modular systems of production are where an organised group of individuals work together to accomplish a common purpose where the team works on one or a few garments at a time and the layout is sequential in a parallel formation where each operator is assigned at least one task or a few adjacent to each other.

Example of detailed operation at each station for the manufacture of a t-shirt in order that the plan is such that it ensures maximum operational and time efficiency

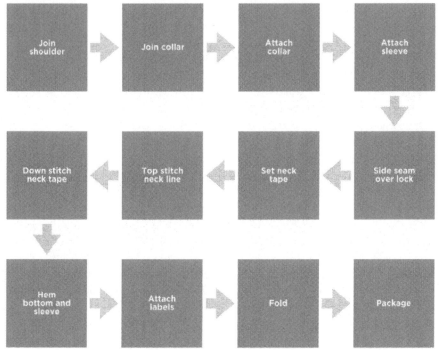

The flow will naturally influence the selection of the production line configuration and in all likelihood the t-shirt will possibly follow the path as illustrated in the first figure above.

Quick response manufacturing

In recent years the substantial shift to high volume cost effective garment off shore manufacturers, the majority of which are based in the East has enforced domestically established suppliers and retailers in traditional manufacturing markets to review their modus operandi in order to keep their plants viable. As a result more and more suppliers are placing emphasis on achieving the benefits of innovation, higher quality and speed in the production cycle where they may be manufacturing in lesser or varying volumes with shorter lead times. This enables them to be nimble enough to react to fashion swings rapidly particularly in an unpredictable market and thereby maintain a competitive advantage.

This objective is assisted by the choice of suitable production process configurations such as cellular groupings with the correct machinery and right attachments such as specialised folders. The needle and thread types should be such that they enable the efficient manufacture of the product type with lower inventory levels and lesser mark downs.

The advantage of quick response manufacturing is that it increases machine up time and therefore delivers an improved quality and subsequently less rework. Where this process is linked to a team incentive programme a consequence is lower staff turnover with fewer social noncompliance issues while also empowering employees and higher productivity.

Typical quick response initiatives is to have product stored at various stages of production so that it is possible to react swiftly to current consumer sales patterns. A prime example is where garments such as knitwear, sweaters, t-shirts, tank tops and the like are made up in uncoloured greige yarn and as the demand happens the garments are then piece dyed to whatever colours the market calls for. Not only in such cases is the benefit of improved sales achieved but it also reduces the build-up of unwanted garments or yarns. Other tactics include the reservation of production capacity but holding back the ordering of fabric and finalisation of the style for as long as possible in order to react more closely to trends as quickly as possible.

The logistics and supply chain functions need to be as streamlined as possible to allow the goods to reach the point of sale as quickly as possible which will require focus on storage, pick and pack operations, format in which the goods are best stored and transported, for example, whether they should be moved in a boxed or in a hanging state where the benefits of speed to market should be offset against the additional costs that will be incurred in setting up a hanging infra-structure.

With the explosion of sophisticated and faster computer systems sales data is transferred in all sorts of variations and is thoroughly analysed in order to rapidly reveal the wants and preferences of consumers that enables quick collaborative decisions and forecast adjustments across the spectrum of mills, suppliers and retailers and through these actions the retailer is able to better serve their customer in a faster time with less product proliferation which increases their competitiveness and offers the opportunity of potential growth of market share.

PACKAGING TECHNOLOGY

The packaging of a product is largely the responsibility of a packaging technologist and plays a critical role in the presentation, protection and communication of information to the consumer as well as taking into account the ecological demands of the environment.

The common purpose of packaging is that it physically protects the product against mechanical shocks, vibrations, varying temperatures, humidity and excessive handling during transit or warehousing. The usual provision of information whether it is on the packaging itself or through the use of labels, indicate any regulations that may apply, the usage and safety instructions, transport guidelines and lists the components and chemicals that were used in the production process.

Packaging assists in the sale of the product in that it serves as a "silent salesman". There is a communication of information through clever graphic design that encompasses the properties of the product, instructions as how to use the merchandise and the provision of safety warnings. Convenience is added by way of easy storage configurations, display conformity and the accommodation of barcoding information which is easily accessible for scanners to capture sales and stock keeping records and store them on a common data base. Specialised packaging plays an important part in securing the product through the use of tamper proof mechanisms and can also be engineered to reduce the pilferage.

Over packaging should be avoided and where possible the utilisation of recycled or recyclable materials in the manufacturing process is encouraged without affecting the functional properties.

Outer cartons must adhere to weight and dimension stipulations and should be able to be easily handled on warehouse equipment such as conveyer belts, pallets and storage slots.

Of the two types, primary packaging enjoys the journey of the product right to the end user while secondary packaging is that which is discarded at various points during the journey.

Examples of primary packaging are self- adhesive tickets which carry the barcode detail, price, reference numbers, colour and size as well as date codes. Swing tickets are used where adhesive tickets are not appropriate and may also be independently attached in order to highlight any unique features of the product. Invariably adhesive tickets are applied to presentation packs, wallets and plastic bags.

Sew in labels are typically a satin tape which is sewn into the garment side or neck seam and carry wash care instructions, product reference numbers, size information, fabric composition, country of origin as well as safety instructions. The fibre content must be described by its generic name but may be accompanied by a brand name or a trade mark. An example would be where woollen products will display the wool mark for which the supplier will have qualified to utilise through their manufacturing process.

An example of garment care and reference label

EXAMPLE OF A GARMENT CARE AND REFERENCE LABEL

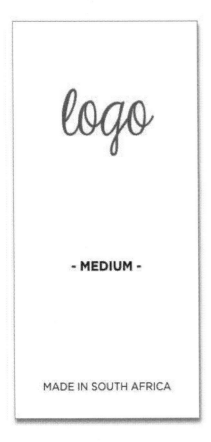

Care markings are not legally required but are commonly indicated by the universal symbols that are consistent and accurate, for example, where a garment needs to be hand washed only and not machine washed it will be highlighted using the relevant symbol

Universal care instruction symbols are key to the garment label and the most common are outlined below

Symbol	Description	Symbol	Description
(60°)	WASHING WATER TEMPERATURE	⊠	DO NOT TUMBLE DRY
(hand)	HAND WASH ONLY	⊘	DRIP DRY IN SHADE
⎍	WASH ON SENSITIVE PROGRAMMES	[‖]	DRIP DRY
⊠	DO NOT WASH	[–]	DRY FLAT
Ⓟ	DRY CLEANABLE	⌂	DRY ON HANGER
⊗	DO NOT DRY CLEAN	⊠	DO NOT IRON
⊠	DO NOT USE BLEACH	⌢	IRON WITH WARM IRON
⊠	DO NOT TUMBLE DRY	⌢	IRON WITH HOT IRON

Country of origin is displayed on labels to indicate geographically where the significant stage of production took place. In most countries this is a legal requirement even if the garment may have some components that originate from other parts of the world. Apart from it being law, the identification gives the consumer the choice of which countries that they may wish to support or not support for political or emotional reasons and participate in buy local promotional campaigns that are designed to stimulate local employment.

Swing tags that describe features or unique properties of products have to be truthful in terms of fit for purpose and of the quality standard that is expected by the customer. Where the product does not meet these claims they can be deemed to be misleading and could have legal implications that can be enforced either by the user or competitors who may feel unfairly disadvantaged. An example of this could be that where a ticket describes the garment as being non-iron but after a few washes it has to be ironed.

Secondary packaging are items such as outer cartons, over bags for hanging product, hanger size indicators, stock room and store address labels, the outer carton product detail and supplier detail stamps.

The procuring and specifying of ecologically friendly packaging should always be done keeping the safety of the environs top of mind. Printing should be done keeping volatile compound emissions to a minimum through, for example, the use of vegetable based ink that are free from heavy metals.

Measures need to be put in place to keep waste of inks, ink tins, and paper to a minimum and the cleaning and recirculation of polluted water should be promoted. Paper packaging and corrugated cartons ought to contain a percentage of recycled papers and must not to have been bleached using chlorine. Plastic packaging should be of recyclable materials such as polypropylene and polyethylene.

Costings

It goes without saying that cost forms an integral part of the negotiation process. It is therefore imperative that the retailer has a good understanding of the components and the proportions of a costing sheet thus permitting the ability to test the validity and understanding of any costing presented by a supplier.

The cost of a product is broken down into two distinct categories, namely direct product costs and the costs associated in getting the completed product to the retailer.

Factors that will influence the cost of a product will be the size ratio, which if weighted towards the larger sizes will utilise more fabric or affect the wastage of fabric because of a less efficient marking of the lay of fabric on the cutting table.

The level of detail of the styling may not only affect fabric consumption, it will probably also influence the manufacture time or minute rating.

The width of the fabric can also affect the usage of fabric and the general rule is that the narrower the width of fabric the more expensive the product is likely to be. Specialist fabrics tend to be on narrow width such as 110cm while the full width is 148cm. Woven fabrics can be as wide as 160cm.

Plain or printed fabrics will also affect fabric usage particularly where stripes need to be matched on different components such as sleeve and body and is likely to result in more wastage of fabric.

The components of the cost of the products can be divided into those that are considered to be fixed such as raw materials, overheads which include services such as design, technology and logistics and those that are variable which are in the main the constituents that are squeezed down to meet the demands of the retailer like wages, working hours and production methods.

Packaging costs will also vary for different types of product. The size of the cartons required to transport the product is determined by the dimensions of height and width that must protect and accommodate the garment comfortably. The in store presentation requirements will also affect the overall cost from the point of view that allowance may be needed for hangers as well as additional swing tickets.

Where goods are imported, duties need to be taken into consideration. Duties are normally determined against the free on board value or in other words the cost to place it on the deck of the ship. They can also be calculated as ex works which is the cost as at the completion of production.

Exchange rates are a critical factor. The option to purchase currency ahead of time at a fixed rate to finance the cost provides the peace of mind that the costs will be stable even if the day to day rates fluctuate. If currency is not bought ahead but goods are purchased at the prevailing rates the retailer may be forced to revise selling prices to ensure the achievement of the target margin.

Different categories of products attract different tariff duties at the receiving country depending on country of origin and manufacture as well as protection policies of local production.

The cost to transport the goods from the place of manufacture will vary for local goods or from the port by the clearing agent, depending on the location of the retailer in relation to the supplier or port, the size of the cartons or container and the mode of transport. Included in this section would be freight and warehousing charges.

The typical elements of a product costing and examples of approximate proportions will be

ELEMENT	DEPENDENCY	CATEGORY
TRANSPORT 5%	Different methods of transport used.	Transport / landing 20%
DUTY 30 - 40%	Taxes levied against the import of goods as specified by the local government.	
SUPPLIER MARGIN 10%	Supplier margin can vary between 5% and 15%.	Production costs 80%
WASH AND TRIMS 5%	Costs allocated to special processes or trims.	
PACKAGING 7%	Total cost of all packaging, including presentation.	
LABOUR 28%	The standard minute rates will differ from country to country, depending on operational complexity.	
FABRIC AND MATERIAL 50%	Will be influenced by the garment rating, which will dictate how much fabric is used to manufacture the garment.	

In addition to the product costs as outlined above there are other costs that need to be taken into account in order to get product to market. These can be categorised basically into two categories, firstly being additional costs to the supplier such as the base overhead costs being the total for rent, electricity, administration costs and the like that will always be there and which must be apportioned per product unit.

The second category can be described as being unrelated to the product directly that have to be paid. The main type of such costs are settlement discount agreements, marketing contributions, finance costs and royalties. These together with the product costs will deliver the final cost of the garment.

Points to note in the review of costs are in cases where the supplier throws in vague and unsubstantiated reasons to justify increases. It is essential that the retailer tests such requests to ensure they carry merit.

A typical instance is where the statement is made that wages have gone up and a new costing is proposed. A cross check is required to determine the proportion of what labour represents of the total costing. In the above example this would be the 28% for labour and apply the increase to this part and reconcile to the proposal.

Where increases are attributed to material increases an effort should be made to investigate the trend in the industry and do some comparisons even if they may be a bit crude. If your research shows that the increase is not in line with the trend, the supplier should be encouraged to find a better source and not to pass on the cost of their inefficiencies.

The use of exchange rate fluctuations to motivate cost price changes is more easily resolved as the average movement can be tracked over a period of time and applied. It is a possibility that in fact there might have been an improvement. Foreign currency could also have an influence depending at what price the supplier or retailer may have covered forward.

If the retailer's volumes are increasing significantly the opportunity exists to negotiate a discount in cost price to share the benefits of the improved scale of efficiencies. A point to note is that while this practice is not discouraged, the smaller retailer may not be able to finance the larger volumes of product or growth based incentives. Even with the benefit of a greater margin, the viability remains to be dependent on the organic growth of the chain, for example, the addition of new stores in order to accommodate the higher buying volumes.

A costing approach which is often employed by retailers is that of requesting appropriate suppliers to tender for a product. In order that this is done fairly and equitably the exact same specifications need to be provided to the potential suppliers. Cross costing comparison between suppliers is a popular option where there are large programmes up for grabs and is unlikely to be used for once off high fashion inputs.

For a retailer to commit to high volume programmes, it is a key requisite that the potential suppliers fulfil some basic requirements in that they must be financially stable, have a reliable track record in terms of delivery performance, provide consistent quality with up to date compliancy audits and will be able to cope with the required volumes which could include the agreement to hold a minimum stock holding. The supplier should also be flexible enough to be able to make styling changes to the product where necessary.

The key stipulations for use with cross costing or tenders which will be provided is a detailed style sheet, comprehensive specifications of fabric and trims, the garment measurements with the range of sizes, volumes, a target cost price, packaging requirements and packing methods, delivery dates or production flow.

CRITICAL PATH MANAGEMENT

Critical path management is undoubtedly one of the key philosophies that needs to be applied in production management in order to have control and knowledge of the work flow in the production of garments. This achieved by the setting up of a timeline that reflects the anticipated critical deadlines that have to be achieved in order to meet the required delivery date of the order and being completely aware of the impact of late deliveries of fabric and components on the realisation of this objective. Without the knowledge of all statuses the consequence could well be the late deliveries with the application of penalties or even worse the cancellation of orders.

Through the management the entire flow of product workflow through the view of progress from concept to completion allows the effective planning of tasks and reallocation of resources to minimises bottlenecks, identify due dates and milestones as well as highlight areas where attention is required. And thereby keep suppliers on schedule as well as encourages collaboration between the different teams. A major benefit is that critical path management allows management to move away from day to day reactive management into a more strategic management role aligned with strategic business objectives.

Ideally a critical path management tool should possess characteristics such as flexibility that enables the tool to be configured to meet the customised requirements of the user. Alerts should be built in to notify stakeholders directly through SMS, emails or pings and Information should be able to be automatically rolled up with an analytical ability to be able to drill down to prescribed levels or issues.

The interface ought to be user friendly and easy to learn, easy to update and where web based tools exist they should be compatible and easily accessible within a range of internet speeds, browsers and levels of internet sophistication that allows global interaction with suppliers in order to track the progress of the product from the sampling stage through to delivery. As supply chains grow in complexity with increased production volumes and links in the supply chain information visibility is imperative in order to facilitate complete transparency while also highlighting the ramifications of poor decision making and poor capacity management.

Some of the software tools that are available in the market place which assist in the monitoring of production progress and are accessible to all stakeholders do come at a cost and albeit expensive the benefits of the investment may well be justified.

Alternatively if the product is too expensive it is well worth developing one's own instrument even though the tool may well be cumbersome and more complex to apply but at least it will provide rough idea of the lead times required for the procurement of fabrics and components for the completion of orders and therefore In order to guarantee the on time launch of the product and the management of the path of product development. Without this the retailer ends up flying blind and often only finds out about delays from the supplier close to the expected delivery date when it is invariably too late to take corrective action. It is not uncommon to hear of the cancellation of large volume contracts worth great values as a result of the relatively low cost care labels not being available on time and thus the completion of the delivery date is compromised. It is not only the physical components that can cause issues the added value outsourced services such as embroideries, pattern making or packaging can in the same manner impact the delivery status if they are not completed on time.

Unfortunately with multiple versions of documents such as cost sheets, design samples and supplier scorecards in differing formats which provide an inadequate platform to share information can result in a lack of awareness into potential supply chain problems and an inability to provide early warnings and synchronise real time responsiveness.

All stakeholders involved in the process, which includes the buyers, suppliers, product technologists, fabric technologists and commercial management need to focus on the critical path management of the product.

The key stages or milestones which are in the main controlled by the buyers and technologists that need to be scrutinised are the style briefing and finalisation, colour approval, fit approval, bulk test of fabrics and components, approval of the pre-production sample, pre-production meetings with the supplier and final approval of the pre-shipment or rail sample prior to production at which point the product development can be considered complete and the launch date is able to be confirmed.

The monitoring of the process needs to documented and highlighted in some form in order that key players are able to measure the actual accomplishment of tasks compared to the required completion dates. If collaboration and communication is ineffective, bottlenecks are likely to occur, production and delivery deadlines may be missed, and penalties will be applied with the resultant squeezing of margins. The purpose of such reports is not only to ensure that the critical milestones are met on time but also serve as a reference for meetings to identify possible delays and decide what actions need to be taken to improve or correct the situation.

In principle the lead times are measured in weeks and the relevant dates are attached starting from launch date which represents zero days and progressively working backwards taking the time for the completion of each stage into account and ending up where the no later than date for the starting style brief stage is determined.

The format of the critical path action plan may well vary from retailer to retailer dependant on the level of detail the measurement takes place in terms of each operation.

The hierarchy of the reporting and performance measurement is usually done at style level and all the styles for a department can be rolled up to departmental level and then up to group level. These together with supplier extracts and other filters make for effective performance management of both the retail teams and the supplier.

An example of a basic critical path management tool which highlights the key milestones, time line and progress monitoring with analytical properties is illustrated below.

PRODUCT DEVELOPMENT MANAGEMENT						Style Brief		Style Finalised		Colour Approved		Fit Approved	
Supplier	Grp	Dept.	Style	Colour	Total	Complete	In-complete	Complete	In-complete	Complete	In-complete	Complete	In-complete
abcd	1	123	44445	Black	Units 1000	900	100	800	200	900	100	750	250
					% 100	90%	10%	80%	20%	90%	10%	75%	25%
					Weeks 39			28		24		11	
					Date 10-Oct			17-Dec		15-Jan		15-Apr	
Supplier	Grp	Dept.	Style	Colour	Total	Complete	In-complete	Complete	In-complete	Complete	In-complete	Complete	In-complete
abcd	1	123	55555	White	Units 1500	1300	200	1400	100	1450	50	1500	0
					% 100	87%	13%	93%	7%	97%	3%	100%	0%
					Weeks 39			28		24		11	
					Date 10-Oct			17-Dec		15-Jan		15-Apr	
Supplier	Grp	Dept.	Style	Colour	Total	Complete	In-complete	Complete	In-complete	Complete	In-complete	Complete	In-complete
bcde	2	124	55556	Yellow	Units 2000	1500	500	1400	600	1600	400	1800	200
					% 100	75%	25%	70%	30%	80%	20%	90%	10%
					Weeks 39			28		24		11	
					Date 10-Nov			17-Jan		15-Feb		15-May	
Supplier	Grp	Dept.	Style	Colour	Total	Complete	In-complete	Complete	In-complete	Complete	In-complete	Complete	In-complete
cdef	3	128	44445	Green	Units 1000	700	300	900	100	800	200	750	250
					% 100	70%	30%	90%	10%	80%	20%	75%	25%
					Weeks 39			28		24		11	
					Date 10-Dec			17-Feb		15-Mar		15-Jun	

PRODUCT DEVELOPMENT MANAGEMENT							Pre-production sample & supplier meeting		Pre-shipment sample		Launch Date	
Supplier	Grp	Dept.	Style	Colour		Total	Complete	In-complete	Complete	In-complete	Complete	In-complete
abcd	1	123	44445	Black	Units	1000	750	250	750	250	750	250
					%	100	75%	25%	75%	25%	75%	25%
					Weeks	39	8		2		0	
					Date	10-Oct	06-May		17-Jun		01-Jul	
Supplier	Grp	Dept.	Style	Colour		Total	Complete	In-complete	Complete	In-complete	Complete	In-complete
abcd	1	123	55555	White	Units	1500	1500	0	1450	50	1500	0
					%	100	100%	0%	97%	3%	100%	0%
					Weeks	39	8		2		0	
					Date	10-Oct	06-May		17-Jun		01-Jul	
Supplier	Grp	Dept.	Style	Colour		Total	Complete	In-complete	Complete	In-complete	Complete	In-complete
bcde	2	124	55556	Yellow	Units	2000	1800	200	1700	300	1900	100
					%	100	90%	10%	85%	15%	95%	5%
					Weeks	39	8		2		0	
					Date	10-Nov	06-Jun		17-Jul		01-Aug	
Supplier	Grp	Dept.	Style	Colour		Total	Complete	In-complete	Complete	In-complete	Complete	In-complete
cdef	3	128	44445	Green	Units	1000	850	150	950	50	950	50
					%	100	85%	15%	95%	5%	95%	5%
					Weeks	39	8		2		0	
					Date	10-Dec	06-Jul		17-Aug		01-Sep	

QUALITY MANAGEMENT

Quality is defined as the combination of design and properties that are required at an acceptable level to perform the ideal form and function requisite to serve the market for which it is intended. In the textile and apparel industry the quality is calculated in terms of quality and standard of fibres, yarns, fabric construction, colour fastness and the final finished product.

Quality control starts with ensuring that the fabric being utilised meets the required specifications to be transformed into a perfect garment and therefore needs to be managed and inspected for faults which are marked. The length and width of fabric have to be checked to ensure that they meet the specified measurements and thereby do not affect the cutting table lay. It is important that the fabric is inspected upon receipt and meets the finished width and stability while the garment must be sound with regards to seam construction and the stitch forming action.

The supplier will need to have the fabric and trims tested by a recognised laboratory to record that they meet the weight, width and yarn specifications. Tests also need to focus on the performance of fabrics such as rub tests or how the fabric reacts in a washing machine in terms of colour fastness and shrinkage.

In the manufacture of garments the objective is to achieve the right final product on time. The final product specifications are dependent on the level of the quality control present in sampling and development departments that from samples to completed production, including layout and process stipulations, the construction parameters and measurement of performance. In order that this done effectively robust recording systems should be in place as well as checklists for the supervisors to logically ensure that all critical points are covered and are within the set down tolerance levels are measured as per performance analysis and reporting. Reporting will outline results of quality control during garment assembly, number of marks and stains on garments, analysis of the cost of faults and directives as how to improve garment cleanliness.

It is vital that proper quality control is applied in order that the product presents well on the shop floor, fits well, wears well, washes well, is functional and represents value for money to avoid the loss of sales through customer returns or the depletion of units during production which results in under deliveries and ultimately lost sales. The points of quality control are conducted throughout the supply chain process which includes those prior to production, during in line production, at dispatch stage and on the shop sales floor.

A quality controller needs to possess certain abilities that will equip them to ensure that a thorough and complete monitor is done. The key attribute required is that of the need to pay attention to detail along with assertiveness and transparency. Tasks have to be conducted professionally and ethically. The incumbent must be prepared to be open minded and consider alternative points of view. The nature of the job requires tact and diplomacy and in certain situations the quality controller is required to be culturally sensitive. Decisiveness together with collaboration is paramount to ensure that quality standards are maximised.

The various steps of quality control and types of checks in the manufacturing process is illustrated below

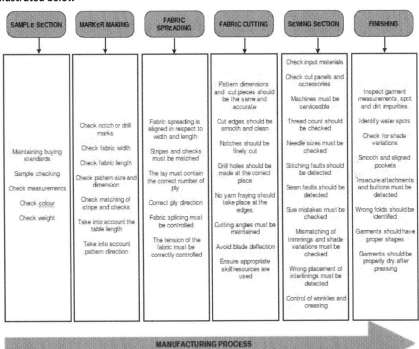

The purpose of the pre-production meeting conducted for every style is to set the standards to which the quality will be measured during production.

The pre-production sample serves as the basis of discussion and all key stakeholders will be present from both the retailer and the supplier. Technology representatives and the buying team must attend together with supplier teams to determine the criteria for sewing, finishing, fabric, trim, quality assurance, cutting, production and packaging management. At these meetings the technical requirements are stipulated and agreed for the make-up, sewing and thread combinations, the special methods that are needed to handle trims in bulk production, the wash and product finishing standards as well as the packaging and shipment methods. Any special processes out of the ordinary must be well documented and the minutes of the meeting must be recorded and signed off by all participants to ensure there are clear reference standards in the event of any difference that may transpire at a later stage.

If required it may be decided to produce wearer trials to assess the performance of the product in relation to the technological test standards especially where physical or chemical laboratory tests are not appropriate or it is not able to be spot checked in bulk production. All in all the purpose of the pre-production meeting is to identify risk areas which may result in product failure or possible injury to the customer and establish preventative measures.

During production the quality audits must include the assessment of care labels, packaging, price tags, colour and the quality of garment finishing and conformance to measurement specifications. The main visual checks will include the button attachments, non-inclusions of seams, fabric flaws, elastic failures, colour mismatches, poor make up and appearance, sew ability of threads have to be checked to ensure there are no broken threads, evidence of skipped stitches and that the stitch spacing is balanced. Safety issues such as needle points or staples in the product are also watched out for.

Final inspection will include will focus on ensuring the consistent colour shading of all parts of the garment, that the garment is balanced in terms of collar, pockets and cuff attachments as well as the critical measurements and weight are within the acceptable tolerances and that all accessories are securely applied and are functional.

It is important that the audit report is completed speedily in order that preventative measures can be documented and action plans are implemented. The number of garments that must be measured and assessed is determined by agreeing the sample survey percentage that will represent the total quantity and what tolerances are allowed before rejection takes place.

The amount to be inspected may vary from no inspection to 100% inspection and may or may not include random inspections. Statistical sampling may be determined that would represent the amount that could be extrapolated to be the character of the total quantity.

It is assumed that 5000 pieces are purchased with the breakdown and sample survey quantities as follows

	WHITE	BLACK
SIZE M	1 500	1 200
SIZE L	1 500	800

Of the 5 000 units, it is agreed to check 30% visually and measure 10%

VISUALLY INSPECTED	WHITE	BLACK
SIZE M	450	360
SIZE L	450	240

MEASURED	WHITE	BLACK
SIZE M	150	120
SIZE L	150	80

Graphically the inspection sample can be depicted as follows

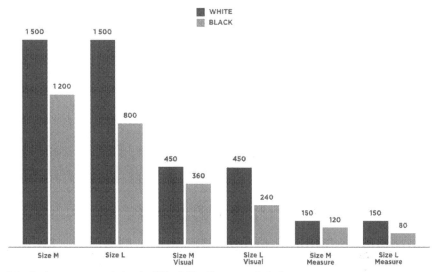

A typical measurement sheet will look like the example below

QUALITY MEASUREMENT AUDIT REPORT												
DEPARTMENT	XYZ	STYLE	STYLE DESCRIPTION									
COLOUR	WHITE	SIZE	SMALL			MEDIUM			LARGE			
OP NO	DESCRIPTION		SPEC (cm)	1	2	3	SPEC (cm)	1	2	3	SPEC (cm)	1	2	3
1	Across front		35				37.5				40			
2	1/2 chest		48				53				56			
3	1/2 hem		46				51				53			
4	Shoulder		13.5				14				16			
5	Overarm sleeve		18				21				23			
6	Underarm sleeve		7.5				9				11			
7	Across back		38				40				43			
8	Neck drop front		8.2				9.5				11			
9	Neck width		18.2				19				21			
10	Neck drop back		1.5				2				2.5			
INSPECTED BY			TOTAL MEASURED				COMMENTS						
			RESULTS										
SUPPLIER			Out of tolerance										
			In tolerance										

In addition to the production line audits it is also necessary to conduct quality inspection in stores which apart from identifying and resolving quality issues there is the added advantage of interacting with sales teams and share knowledge and learnings from those at the coal face who interact with the customer.

Apart from the skill levels and components which may affect the quality of a garment there are other factors which need to be taken into account. For Chinese suppliers it is important to consider production which takes place close to the Chinese New Year holidays. Not only is it the completion of orders prior to the commencement of holidays which could put pressure on the rate of production the other real risk is the start-up time taken by factories after the holidays. This is often a slow process due to the fact that many of the workers who travel inland to their villages are tardy in returning back to work or take extended leave which results in broken production and the use of lower skill levels to complete more complex operations. This phenomenon is part and parcel of doing business with Chinese suppliers and contingencies need to be put in place as invariably suppliers who do not have the capacity to complete orders on time which were optimistically accepted as well as the fact that raw material suppliers experience the same phenomenon also puts excessive strain on the production lines to meet deadlines timeously. In summary careful planning with built in safety stocks to ensure continuity of supply to the stores is paramount.

Environmental circumstances such as storms which prevent ships docking or deviate from their routes, power failures, strikes, goods being held up at customs or other unforeseen events can delay the arrival of raw materials and finished product and may impact eventually on the timing, quality and quantity being delivered.

CONCLUSION

Healthy partnerships between the retailer and the supplier is an essential pre-requisite to ensure the success of both parties. From get go there has to be a circle of trust to promote collaboration and mutual respect. As has been highlighted frequently the only guarantee about change is that there will be change and it is without doubt that the retailers' greatest ally when change happens, whether it be positive or negative, is their source of supply. The support of the supplier through their flexibility and ability to appreciate the need for revolution is vital for the shared destiny and the celebration of success for both businesses.

The sourcing setting has evolved into a highly complex process environment, where the multiple processes, functions and suppliers in many different factories need to collaborate and work together in such a way in order to produce products in as short as time as possible. The seamless integration of roles and activities of all stakeholders is essential to ensure that the end objective of servicing the customer with the highest quality product that is fully functional which effectively meets the consumer's aspirations and expectations in terms of style, price and consistent availability.

Hopefully the book has achieved the objective of entrenching the realisation of the critical need to mesh the activities of the multiple stakeholders in such a way that they are aligned with a common purpose and the successful end result is perceived by the customer to be the work of one united unit.

Made in the USA
Columbia, SC
11 January 2022

54120557R00033